THE 5
LEVELS OF
LEADERSHIP

Books by Dr. John C. Maxwell
Can Teach You How to Be a REAL Success

Relationships

25 Ways to Win with People

Becoming a Person of Influence

Encouragement Changes Everything

Ethics 101

Everyone Communicates,
Few Connect

The Power of Partnership

Relationships 101

Winning with People

Attitude

Attitude 101

The Difference Maker

Failing Forward

How Successful People Think

Sometimes You Win—
Sometimes You Learn

Success 101

Thinking for a Change

The Winning Attitude

Equipping

The 15 Invaluable Laws of Growth

The 17 Essential Qualities
of a Team Player

The 17 Indisputable Laws
of Teamwork

Developing the Leaders Around You

Equipping 101

Make Today Count

Mentoring 101

My Dream Map

Partners in Prayer

Put Your Dream to the Test

Running with the Giants

Talent Is Never Enough

Today Matters

Your Road Map for Success

Leadership

The 5 Levels of Leadership

The 10th Anniversary Edition
of The 21 Irrefutable Laws
of Leadership

The 21 Indispensable Qualities
of a Leader

The 21 Most Powerful Minutes
in a Leader's Day

The 360 Degree Leader

Developing the Leader
Within You

Go for Gold

How Successful People Lead

Leadership 101

Leadership Gold

Leadership Promises for
Every Day

THE
5
LEVELS
OF
LEADERSHIP

PROVEN STEPS TO MAXIMIZE
YOUR POTENTIAL

JOHN C. MAXWELL

**CENTER
STREET**

NEW YORK   BOSTON   NASHVILLE

The author is represented by Yates & Yates, LLP,
Literary Agency, Orange, California.

Scripture taken from the New King James Version (NKJV). Copyright © 1982 by Thomas Nelson, Inc. Used by permission. All rights reserved.

Scripture taken from the New American Standard Bible® (NASB), Copyright © 1960, 1962, 1963, 1968, 1971, 1972, 1973, 1975, 1977, 1995 by The Lockman Foundation. Used by permission.

Center Street
Hachette Book Group
1290 Avenue of the Americas
New York, NY 10104

www.CenterStreet.com

Printed in the United States of America

LSC-C

First trade edition: September 2013
18

Center Street is a division of Hachette Book Group, Inc.
The Center Street name and logo are trademarks of
Hachette Book Group, Inc.

The Hachette Speakers Bureau provides a wide range of authors for speaking events. To find out more, go to www.HachetteSpeakersBureau.com or call (866) 376-6591.

The publisher is not responsible for websites (or their content) that are not owned by the publisher.

The Library of Congress has cataloged the hardcover edition as follows:

Maxwell, John C., 1947-
   The five levels of leadership : proven steps to maximize your potential / John C. Maxwell. — 1st ed.
      p. cm.
ISBN 978-1-59995-365-6
   1. Leadership.   I. Title.   II. Title: 5 levels of leadership.
   HD57.7.M3936 2011
   658.4'092 — dc22   2011004785

ISBN 978-1-59995-363-2 (pbk.)

This book is dedicated to EQUIP (www.iequip.org)
and all the people who are a part of this
leadership organization. EQUIP's Rule of 5:
Every day we…

1. Think Globally
2. Evaluate Our Leadership Strategy
3. Create Resources
4. Develop Associate Trainers, Partners, and Donors
5. Train Leaders to Train Leaders

Millions of Leaders are being trained
because of your efforts. Thanks!

Contents

Acknowledgments

Thank you to:
Charlie Wetzel, my writer;
Stephanie Wetzel, my social media manager;
Linda Eggers, my executive assistant.

You Can Have a Leadership Game Plan for Your Life

Leadership is one of my passions. So is teaching it. I've dedicated more than thirty years of my life to helping others learn what I know about leading. In fact, I spend about eighty days every year teaching leadership. In the last several years, I've taught about it on six continents. The subject is inexhaustible. Why? Because everything rises and falls on leadership. If you want to make a positive impact on the world, learning to lead better will help you do it.

In all the years that I've taught about leadership, there has been one lecture that I have been asked to give more often than any other—from West Point to Microsoft and in countries all around the world. That lecture explains how leadership works, and it provides a game plan for learning how to become a leader. It's "The 5 Levels of Leadership."

My belief that everything rises and falls on leadership solidified in 1976, and it set me on a leadership journey that I am still traveling to this day. I began the journey by asking many questions. *How do you*

define leadership? What is a leader? How does leadership work?
Unfortunately, people's usual answers to those questions are not very helpful. Some people identify leadership with obtaining a leadership position. But I've known bad leaders who had good positions and good leaders who had no position at all. Haven't you? Other people say of leadership, "I can't describe it, but I know it when I see it." While that may be true, it doesn't help anyone learn how to lead.

The conclusion I came to early on is that leadership is influence. If people can increase their influence with others, they can lead more effectively. As I reflected on that, a concept for how leadership works began to crystallize in my mind. That concept was the 5 Levels of Leadership, which took me about five years to develop. I have been teaching it ever since. And whenever I present it, one of the questions people always ask is, "When are you going to write a book about this?" As you can see, I'm finally answering that question.

You Can Learn Practical Leadership Tools

There are a lot of books about leadership lining people's bookshelves. Why should you read this one? Because it works. The 5 Levels has been used to train leaders in companies of every size and configuration, from small businesses to Fortune 100 companies. It has been used to help nonprofit organizations understand how to lead volunteers. And it's been taught in more than 120 countries around the world. Every time I talk about it, people ask questions and make observations. Those things have helped the 5 Levels of Leadership to become stronger and to develop greater depth. The concept is tested and proven. In addition, it offers several other benefits:

The 5 Levels of Leadership Provides a Clear Picture of Leadership

How do people get a handle on leadership? For those who are not naturally gifted for it, leadership can be a mystery. For them, leading people is like walking down a dark corridor. They have a sense of where they want to go, but they can't see ahead and they don't know where the problems and pitfalls are going to lie. For many people in the academic world, leadership is a theoretical exercise, an equation whose variables are worthy of research, study, and rigorous debate. In contrast, the 5 Levels of Leadership is visually straightforward, so anyone can learn it.

The 5 Levels of Leadership Defines *Leading* as a Verb, Not a Noun

Leadership is a process, not a position. There was a time when people used the terms *leadership* and *management* interchangeably. I think most people now recognize that there is a significant difference between the two. Management is at its best when things stay the same.

> Leadership is a process, not a position.

Leadership deals with people and their dynamics, which are continually changing. They are never static. The challenge of leadership is to create change and facilitate growth. Those require movement, which, as you will soon see, is inherent in moving up from one level of leadership to the next.

The 5 Levels of Leadership Breaks Down Leading into Understandable Steps

The subject of leadership can be overwhelming and confusing. Where does leadership start? What should we do first? What processes should we use? How can we gain influence with others? How can we develop a productive team? How do we help followers become leaders in their own right? The 5 Levels of Leadership gives answers to these questions using understandable steps.

The 5 Levels of Leadership Provides a Clear Game Plan for Leadership Development

Too often when people think of their journey into leadership, they envision a career path. What they should be thinking about is their own leadership development! Good leadership isn't about advancing yourself. It's about advancing your team. The 5 Levels of Leadership provides clear steps for leadership growth. Lead people well and help members of your team to become effective leaders, and a successful career path is almost guaranteed.

The 5 Levels of Leadership Aligns Leadership Practices, Principles, and Values

When I developed the 5 Levels, I conceived of each level as a practice that could be used to lead more effectively. As time went by and I used and taught the levels, I realized they were actually principles. Here's the difference: a practice is an action that may work in one situation but not necessarily in another. A principle is an external truth that is as reliable as a physical law. For example, when Solomon said, "A gentle answer turns away every wrath, but a harsh word stirs up anger," he stated a principle that is universal and timeless. Principles are important because they function like a map, allowing us to make wise decisions. If we embrace a principle and internalize it, it becomes a part of our values. The 5 Levels influences my leadership life every day.

Overview of the 5 Levels of Leadership

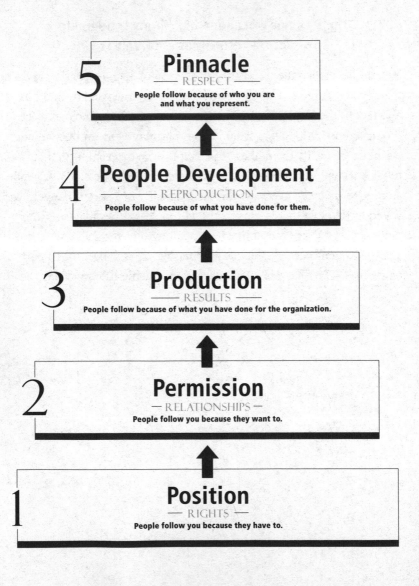

5 **Pinnacle**
— RESPECT —
People follow because of who you are and what you represent.

4 **People Development**
— REPRODUCTION —
People follow because of what you have done for them.

3 **Production**
— RESULTS —
People follow because of what you have done for the organization.

2 **Permission**
— RELATIONSHIPS —
People follow you because they want to.

1 **Position**
— RIGHTS —
People follow you because they have to.

Each of the subsequent sections of this book is dedicated to one of the 5 Levels. In them you will learn the upside of the level, the downside, the best behaviors for that level, the beliefs that help a leader move up to the next level, and how the level relates to the Laws of Leadership. If you are already familiar with the Laws of Leadership, your understanding will be enhanced by seeing how they fit in the 5 Levels. But even if you are new to the laws, you will understand the basic concept behind each and how it is applicable. There is also a growth guide for each level. However, before we dive into the levels, I want to give you an overview of them and how they fit together, as well as share some insights about the levels.

Level 1—Position

Position is the lowest level of leadership—the entry level. The only influence a positional leader has is that which comes with the job title. People follow because they have to. Positional leadership is based on the *rights* granted by the position and title. Nothing is wrong with having a leadership position. Everything is wrong with using position to get people to follow. Position is a poor substitute for influence.

People who make it only to Level 1 may be bosses, but they are never leaders. They have subordinates, not team members. They rely on rules, regulations, policies, and organization charts to control their people. Their people will only follow them within the stated boundaries of their authority. And their people will usually do only what is required of them. When positional leaders ask for extra effort or time, they rarely get it.

Positional leaders usually have difficulty working with volunteers, younger people, and the highly educated. Why? Because positional leaders have no influence, and these types of people tend to be more independent.

Position is the only level that does not require ability and effort to achieve. Anyone can be appointed to a position.

Level 2—Permission

Level 2 is based entirely on *relationships*. On the Permission level, people follow because they want to. When you like people and treat them like individuals who have value, you begin to develop influence with them. You develop trust. The environment becomes much more positive—whether at home, on the job, at play, or while volunteering.

The agenda for leaders on Level 2 isn't preserving their position. It's getting to know their people and figuring out how to get along with them. Leaders find out who their people are. Followers find out who their leaders are. People build solid, lasting relationships.

> You can like people without leading them, but you cannot lead people well without liking them.

You can like people without leading them, but you cannot lead people well without liking them. That's what Level 2 is about.

Level 3—Production

One of the dangers of getting to the Permission level is that a leader may be tempted to stop there. But good leaders don't just create a pleasant working environment. They get things done! That's why they must move up to Level 3, which is based on *results*. On the Production level leaders gain influence and credibility, and people begin to follow them because of what they have done for the organization.

Many positive things begin happening when leaders get to Level 3. Work gets done, morale improves, profits go up, turnover goes down, and goals are achieved. It is also on Level 3 that momentum kicks in.

Leading and influencing others becomes fun on this level. Success and productivity have been known to solve a lot of problems. As legendary former NFL quarterback Joe Namath said, "When you're winning, nothing hurts."

On Level 3, leaders can become change agents. They can tackle tough problems and face thorny issues. They can make the difficult decisions that will make a difference. They can take their people to another level of effectiveness.

Level 4—People Development

Leaders become great, not because of their power, but because of their ability to empower others. That is what leaders do on Level 4. They use their position, relationships, and productivity to invest in their followers and develop them until those followers become leaders in their own right. The result is *reproduction*; Level 4 leaders reproduce themselves.

Production may win games, but People Development wins championships. Two things always happen on Level 4. First, teamwork goes to a very high level. Why? Because the high

> Leaders become great, not because of their power, but because of their ability to empower others.

investment in people deepens relationships, helps people to know one another better, and strengthens loyalty. Second, performance increases. Why? Because there are more leaders on the team, and they help to improve everybody's performance.

Level 4 leaders change the lives of the people they lead. Accordingly, their people follow them because of what their leaders have done for them personally. And their relationships are often lifelong.

Level 5—Pinnacle

The highest and most difficult level of leadership is the Pinnacle. While most people can learn to climb to Levels 1 through 4, Level 5 requires not only effort, skill, and intentionality, but also a high level of talent. Only naturally gifted leaders ever make it to this highest level. What do leaders do on Level 5? They develop people to become Level 4 leaders.

If people are respectful, pleasant, and productive, they can establish a degree of influence with others and gain followers with relative ease. Developing followers to lead on their own is difficult. Most leaders don't do it because it takes so much more work than simply leading followers. However, developing leaders to the point where they are able and willing to develop other leaders is the most difficult leadership task of all. But here are the payoffs: Level 5 leaders develop Level 5 organizations. They create opportunities that other leaders don't. They create legacy in what they do. People follow them because of who they are and what they represent. In other words, their leadership gains a positive *reputation*. As a result, Level 5 leaders often transcend their position, their organization, and sometimes their industry.

Insights into the 5 Levels
of Leadership

Now that you are acquainted with the levels, I want to share some insights that will help you to understand how the levels relate to one another.

1. You Can Move Up a Level But You Never Leave
the Previous One Behind

Now that you've seen the levels and learned the basics about them, you may assume that a leader climbs them, leaving one to arrive at the next, similar to the way one moves up a staircase. But the truth is that you never leave a level behind after you've achieved it. Instead, you simply build upon it. If you think about it for a moment, you'll agree that it makes sense. If you start out with a leadership position and you build relationships with the people you oversee, do you resign your position to do so? No. You don't leave your position to advance, but if you win Level 2 correctly, you never need to rely on your position again.

Once you've built relationships with people and move to a higher level of productivity, do you abandon or neglect those relationships? You had better not! If you do, you'll find yourself back down at Level 1 again.

Leaders don't trade one level for another. They add a new level to the previous one. It is a building process.

2. You Are Not on the Same Level with Every Person

Leadership is dynamic, and it changes from relationship to relationship. The same is true for the 5 Levels of Leadership. I may be on a different one of the 5 Levels with each of five different people at my job. Someone the first day on the job will acknowledge only my position, while someone in whom I've invested and whom I've raised up to lead will likely put me on Level 4. If I've been a good father at home, I may be on Level 4 with my children. If I've been an absentee dad, I may be on Level 1. With my next-door neighbor, perhaps I'm on Level 2.

Have you ever cast vision with your team and had a variety of responses to the same piece of communication? To what do you attribute that? Different backgrounds of the listeners? Different intelligence levels? Different levels of training or experience? Different personalities? I believe all of those factors can come into play, but often the most impacting factor is the level of leadership you're on with each person. People will respond to you based on the level of leadership you're on with them. And that is subject to change.

> People will respond to you based on the level of leadership you're on with them.

Achieving a level of leadership is not like earning a degree. Nor is it like setting a record as an athlete. You don't achieve it and leave it. It's more like having to run a race every day to prove your ability. The lone exception is the Pinnacle. Leaders who rise to Level 5 are sometimes given credit for being on that level by reputation instead of just personal interaction. But it's important to note that at any level, a leader doesn't always automatically stay at that level. You must earn your level of leadership with each person, and that level can go up or down at any time.

3. The Higher You Go, The Easier It Is to Lead

Here's some good news. As you work to climb up the levels of leadership, you'll find that it gets easier to lead people. Each advance allows you to be more effective in leading others because your influence increases as you go to a higher level. As your influence increases, more people follow you more readily. Limited influence, limited leadership. Greater influence, greater effectiveness. That's common sense. However, there's also some bad news: it's not easy to climb the levels of leadership! If it were easy, everyone would be a Level 5 leader.

4. The Higher You Go, the More Time and Commitment Is Required to Win a Level

Which is harder? Being given a leadership position (Level 1) or getting people's permission to lead them (Level 2)? That's pretty obvious. It takes time, effort, and commitment to develop positive relationships with people. How about moving from Level 2 to Level 3? I believe it is harder to become consistently productive than it is to make friends. It's even harder and requires much more time to go to Level 4, where you develop people to become good leaders. And it can take a lifetime to become a Level 5 leader who develops leaders who in turn develop other leaders.

Years ago I remember seeing a *Ziggy* cartoon by Tom Wilson in which the hero of the strip was on the road to success, and up ahead he could see a sign that said, "Prepare to stop for tolls." That would be good advice for anyone wanting to rise up the 5 Levels of Leadership. There is no easy way to get to the top. And each time you go up, you pay. You have to be more committed, you have to give more, you have to use more energy, each time you want to go up a level. And so do your people. Nobody achieves anything great by giving the minimum. No teams win championships without making sacrifices and giving their best.

5. Moving Up Levels Occurs Slowly, But Going Down Can Happen Quickly

As I've said, it takes time to climb up the levels of leadership. I've had people ask me, "How long will it take me to become a Level 5 leader?"

"A lot longer than you think" is my answer. Building always takes a lot longer than destroying. A lot of things have to be right to climb to

> A lot of things have to be right to climb to a higher level, but sometimes it takes only one thing going wrong to cause someone to fall.

a higher level, but sometimes it takes only one thing going wrong to cause someone to fall. For example, think about how long it takes to build a great relationship with a person. But if you do something to lose trust with that person, the relationship can become permanently broken in the blink of an eye.

While it's unsettling to think about how quickly one can fall from a level of leadership, I hope you can take solace in this: once you've climbed up to higher levels, the ones below you function as a safety net. So the more you've advanced up the levels, the more secure your leadership is. For example, if you make some bad decisions on Level 3 that ruin your productivity or that of the team, the relationships you've developed may save you from being fired. The only level without a safety net is the lowest one: Position. You don't get too many chances to make mistakes on that level. That's another good reason to work your way up the levels of leadership.

6. The Higher You Go, the Greater the Return

You may give more to climb to higher levels of leadership, but you get more, too. As a leader, your return on investment increases with each level. On Level 2, you earn trust and the right to lead. On Level 3, you add to the productivity of the organization. On Level 4, you multiply that productivity because every time you add another leader to an organization, you add all the horsepower of that leader's team. On Level 5, the growth and productivity become exponential as you add leaders to the organization who not only lead others but also create generations of leadership development that keep on producing.

The better the leaders are in an organization, the better everyone in the organization becomes. When productivity is high, chemistry is good, morale is high, and momentum is strong, then the payoffs increase.

7. Moving Farther Up Always Requires Further Growth

Each time a leader moves up to a higher level of leadership, greater skill is required. For that reason, each step of growth requires further development on the part of the leader. But here's the good news. Each level of leadership achieved functions as a platform from which the leader can grow into the next.

Here's how this works. To grow to a new level, leaders take risks. At the lower levels, the risks are smaller and more easily won. For example, to make the climb from Level 1 to Level 2, leaders risk initiating relationships. When leaders get to higher levels, the risks get bigger. For example, on Level 3, leaders may rally the team to try to accomplish a lofty goal only to fail; that could cost the leader credibility, stop momentum, and demotivate team members. But here's the good news: every risk at a higher level is a natural extension of the skills that leaders have by then developed. Outsiders might look at a leader and say, "Wow, he really stepped out and took a big risk." But those observers may not see the growth that has occurred in the leader. By the time the next risk must be undertaken, the leader has grown into it.

Growing as a leader requires a combination of intentional growth and leadership experience. If people rely only on

> Growing as a leader requires a combination of intentional growth and leadership experience.

experience without intentionally learning and preparing for the next level, they won't progress as leaders. On the other hand, if they only prepare mentally yet obtain no experience through risk and reward, and trial and error, then they still won't progress. It takes both—plus some amount of talent. But you have no control over how much talent you possess. You control only what you do with it.

You see this dynamic when athletes try to move up from the college ranks to the pros. They all have a degree of talent. What helps those who succeed are intentional growth *and* experience. The athletes who rely only on their college experience often don't make it. And the ones who prepare mentally and physically but never get actual game experience often have the same negative outcome. It takes both to be successful.

If you possess a natural gift for leadership, you probably have a passion for growth. You like to see things build. It's part of your wiring. Go with it. If you have a more modest amount of talent, don't lose hope. You can make up for a lot by becoming a highly intentional student of leadership, thereby making the most of every opportunity. Either way, remember that success at any level helps you to be successful at every level. So work hard to win the level you're on now. It will prepare you for the future.

8. Not Climbing The Levels Limits You and Your People

The Law of the Lid in *The 21 Irrefutable Laws of Leadership* states, "Leadership ability determines a person's level of effectiveness." In short, your effectiveness in getting things done and your ability to work through others is always limited by your leadership. If your leadership is a 4 out of 10, then your effectiveness will be no higher than a 4. Additionally, the Law of Respect says, "People naturally follow leaders stronger than themselves." That means that if you remain a 4, then you will never attract and keep any leaders better than a 3![1]

One of the burdens of leadership is that as we go, so go the people we lead. Reaching our potential sets an environment for others to reach theirs. When leaders stop climbing, two questions need to be asked: "Can they improve?" and "Will they improve?" Some people can't; they've reached their limit. Others won't. Capacity is not the problem: choice and attitude are. If

> One of the burdens of leadership is that as we go, so go the people we lead. Reaching our potential sets an environment for others to reach theirs.

people are willing to choose improvement and change their attitude, the sky is the limit.

Your leadership ability today is whatever it is. You can't change the past. However, you can change the future. You have a choice concerning your leadership ability from this day forward. If you learn to climb the Levels of Leadership, your leadership ability will improve. And that will positively impact your overall leadership capacity. However, if you choose not to grow as a leader, you better get used to being wherever you currently are, because your situation isn't likely to improve.

9. When You Change Positions or Organizations, You Seldom Stay at the Same Level

What happens when leaders make a job change and begin leading a new group of people? If you assumed that they stay on the same Level of Leadership, you are mistaken. Every time you lead different people you start the process over again. People don't recognize you as a Level 4 People Developer when you haven't worked with them. You have to earn that. The same goes for Levels 3 and 2. You start over at Level 1. However, there is good news. If you reached Level 4 with some other group of people, you already know how to get there. And because you've done it before, you can move up the levels much more quickly than the previous time.

Each time you go through the process with a new group of people, you become even more skilled at it. And after you've done it enough times, you won't be discouraged by the prospect of having to repeat it with others. For example, for twenty-five years I led in the religious world. In that time I worked in four different organizations, and in each I had to climb the levels of leadership with the people there. Fortunately, in that world I was able to reach Level 4 with many people, even many who were outside of those particular organizations. However, when I started teaching leadership in the business world, everything changed. I started back at Level 1 with many people. I didn't let that intimidate or discourage me. I was willing to prove myself and work my way up through the levels again. And now, fifteen years later, I'm enjoying the credibility I've earned by developing relationships, being productive in that world, and developing leaders.

Positional leaders are reluctant to have to start over. Because they think of leadership as a destination instead of a process—a noun instead of a verb—they want to hold onto what they have. Their hope is to do it once and be done. Good leaders are willing to re-earn their way back into leadership because they understand that the leadership life will almost always require them to start again at the bottom more than once.

10. You Cannot Climb the Levels Alone

One of my favorite sayings is, "If you think you're leading but no one is following, then you are only taking a walk." That thought captures the true nature of leadership and also expresses the most important insight about the 5 Levels of Leadership. To succeed as a leader, you must help others follow you up the levels. If people aren't following you, you're not moving up from Level 1 to Levels 2 and 3. If other people following you up the levels

> "Leadership is accepting people where they are, then taking them somewhere."
> —C. W. Perry

aren't becoming leaders themselves, then you haven't reached Level 4. And if the people you're developing aren't on Level 4 developing generations of leaders, then you will not achieve Level 5. The entire process includes other people and focuses on helping them. As Quaker leader C. W. Perry said, "Leadership is accepting people where they are, then taking them somewhere." That's what the 5 Levels of Leadership is all about!

It's Time to Go to the Next Level

I trust that you now have a basic understanding of the 5 Levels of Leadership and how it works. But I'm guessing that by now you're asking yourself, *What level am I on with most of my people?* I make this assertion because every time I teach the 5 Levels, that is a question people want answered.

I'll help you to do that in a moment, but first let me say this: understanding the 5 Levels of Leadership and knowing what level you are on with each person will determine how you lead them. Good leaders do not lead everyone the same way. Why? Because every person is different, and you're not on the same level of leadership with every person. Effective leaders interact with followers based on:

- Where they are with that specific follower,
- Where the follower perceives the leader to be, and
- Where the followers are in their own leadership development.

Each of these factors comes into play as you evaluate your leadership and work to develop it.

I believe every person has the ability to improve in leadership. Becoming a leader isn't a mystical subject. It can be approached very practically, and everyone has the potential to move up to a higher level of leadership.

What is your potential? Do you have the capacity and the desire to become a Level 3, 4, or 5 leader? There's only one way to find out. Accept the leadership challenge, give growth your best effort, and dive into leadership. If you're willing to pick up the gauntlet, you'll never regret it, because there is no better way to increase your positive impact on the world and add value to others than to increase your leadership ability.

I believe this book, with its guides for growth at each level, will help you to navigate the process and help you climb. So good reading, good growing, and as my friend Zig Ziglar says, "I'll see you at the top."

Leadership
Assessment

How to Gauge Your Current Level of Leadership

This is a four-part questionnaire to help you understand where you are in the leadership journey related to the 5 Levels. I want to encourage you to stop moving forward in the book and immediately spend the time required to assess your current level. Completing parts 1 and 2 should not require a large investment of your time. Part 3 may take a bit longer, since it involves other people, but please get that started, too. Its main purpose is to verify whether your instincts and self-perception are correct in Part 2. Part 4 will give you insight into where you stand overall with your team and should be done after you've completed parts 1, 2, and 3.

If you do this groundwork, you will be in a much better position to grow in your leadership as you read and work through the remainder of the book.

Part 1 — Leadership Level Characteristics

This first section applies to your leadership in general. Please read the following ten statements. Place a check mark next to each one that you agree is true for you. Answer using your first instinct. Please do not skip any questions, and do not go back and change any of your responses.

Level 1

- ☑ I don't have to remind the people who work for me that I am the leader.
- ☑ I think of each person who works for me as an individual person, not just in terms of his or her function or role.
- ☑ Most days I look forward to going to work.
- ☑ I recognize that the position I've been given is an opportunity to learn, not turf to be guarded.
- ☑ The people who work for me are willing to do work above and beyond their job descriptions.
- ☑ I know that dealing with people problems is a part of leading and have accepted that as part of the job.
- ☑ I possess the desire to learn more about leadership and become a better leader.
- ☐ I think of my job in terms of work to be accomplished and give very little focus to career path and the positions I desire to achieve along the way.
- ☑ One of my primary objectives is to assist the people who work for me.
- ☑ Most people find it easy to work with me.

If you marked eight or more of the previous statements as true for you, then you have probably already established yourself as a leader on Level 1 and have begun to move to the higher levels. Move on to the next section of the test. However, if you checked fewer than eight, then you have probably not yet mastered Level 1, and this is where you will probably begin your work in personal leadership development. Why? Because you are only as good as the lowest level you've mastered.

Level 2

- ☑ People outside of my department or area of responsibility respect my opinions and frequently seek me out for advice.
- ☑ I know my strengths and weaknesses and rarely get blindsided in my work.
- ☑ I genuinely like most people and want to help them.
- ☑ I am very consistent and even-tempered in my interaction with the people who work for me.
- ☑ When I say something to the people on my team, they always know they can count on it because I am trustworthy.
- ☑ I have developed solid relationships with all of the people who work for me.
- ☐ The people who work with me find me likable and pleasant nearly 100 percent of the time.
- ☑ When I need to have a candid conversation with team members to correct errors or take care of problems, I follow through and don't allow too much time to go by.
- ☑ I believe that employees desire more than just a fair day's pay for a fair day's work; most desire encouragement and I give it to them.
- ☑ I have developed relationships with everyone who works for me.

If you marked eight or more of the above statements as true for you, then move on to the next section. If not, you may want to save the rest of Part 1 of the test for later because your answers indicate that you've not yet mastered Level 2 and you don't yet think like a Level 2 leader. If you do decide to complete Part 1 at this time, please be aware that even if you mark eight or more statements true in subsequent sections, you cannot be on the higher levels of leadership because you have not yet won Level 2. This also applies as you answer the questions in subsequent levels.

Level 3

☒ I consistently hit targets and goals in my work.

☒ Good people always want to work with me and my team.

☒ People see me as an expert in my field and seek me out to learn from me.

☒ I am constantly setting and achieving higher goals for myself, even when my superiors don't set them for me.

☒ My performance in my work often carries the team to a higher level.

☒ I give my best to whatever I do.

☒ I am comfortable with the idea that others are watching how I perform and follow my example.

☒ I am known as a problem solver, and I often get difficult tasks done.

☒ My work is very consistent on a daily basis.

☐ I have systems and routines that help me perform at a very high level.

If you marked eight or more of the above statements as true for you, then move on to the next section. If not, your answers indicate that you've not yet mastered Level 3 and you don't yet think like a Level 3 leader.

Level 4

☐ I schedule and follow through with training and development for all the members of my team on a regular, consistent basis.

☒ When deadlines loom or work becomes urgent, we never cancel our training and development sessions.

☐ I consistently take risks by giving people responsibilities and authority that will stretch them.

☐ I spend a significant amount of time every month mentoring up-and-coming leaders.

☒ I know very thoroughly the strengths and weaknesses of all the people I lead.

☐ I individualize the way I train, develop, and mentor my people.

☐ I spend the most strategic and significant mentoring time with the people who have the highest capacity, talent, and potential.

☒ I have a history of moving people from position to position to help find their fit.

☒ I am continually giving people feedback, not just during formal reviews.

☐ My team or department is considered by others to be the best trained (or one of the best) in the organization.

If you marked eight or more of the above statements as true for you, then move on to the next section. If not, your answers indicate that you've not yet mastered Level 4 and you don't yet think like a Level 4 leader.

Level 5

☐ I can name several specific people whom I have encouraged to speak hard truths to me, and they do so regularly.

☐ I am using my influence to instill values in my organization.

- ☐ The course of my organization is set by me or by a team of which I am a part.
- ☐ I have developed many leaders who are developers of leaders.
- ☐ I enjoy the interaction and friendship of a small circle of leaders with whom I am taking the leadership journey.
- ☐ I am still at the top of my game, and the positive impact I am making is strong.
- ☐ I can name at least one person who would be ready to step in and take my place should I decide to leave my current position.
- ☐ I have influence outside of my organization.
- ☐ People from outside of my specific industry seek me out for leadership advice.
- ☐ I am using my influence and resources for causes greater than myself or my organization.

In leadership, you are only as good as the lowest level you've mastered. So I just want to remind you that even if you scored highly in one of the higher levels, if you scored poorly on a lower level, your leadership is actually on that lower level. That is where you will need to give your attention when working with people to improve your leadership ability.

Part 2 — Individual Team Member Assessment — Leader's Point of View

For each person you oversee directly (direct reports), please answer yes or no to the questions on the following worksheet. (Be sure to complete Part 2 before moving on to Part 3.)

INDIVIDUAL TEAM MEMBER ASSESSMENT

Name of Team Member: **Date:**

_____   _____

Level 1

Yes   No   This person acknowledges you as his or her leader.

Yes   No   This person would agree that you are suited for the leadership position you hold.

Yes   No   This person would acknowledge that you see your position as an opportunity to earn your place at the leadership table, not as a privilege to be used for personal advancement.

Level 2

Yes   No   You know things about this person's family and personal life outside of his or her work.

Yes   No   You know this person's strengths and weaknesses.

Yes   No   You know this person's hopes and dreams.

Yes   No   You are committed to helping this person succeed in his or her work.

Yes   No   This person trusts you and you trust him or her.

Level 3

Yes   No   This person respects your professional ability and qualities.

Yes   No   This person asks for your advice and expertise.

Yes   No   This person has become more productive because of your influence.

Yes   No   This person would acknowledge that the team is more productive because of your leadership.

Yes   No   This person would agree that your team contributes to the vision and purpose of the organization.

Level 4

Yes No You have given this person specific training that has helped him or her to perform better.

Yes No You have mentored this person or put him or her in a development process that has helped him or her to become a better leader.

Yes No This person is now leading others because you have given opportunities and training for him or her to lead.

Yes No This person is consistently loyal and supportive, and always gives you the benefit of the doubt.

Level 5

Yes No This person is not only leading others but has trained those he or she leads to develop leaders thanks to your input.

Yes No This person could step into your role with a very high probability of success if you were to step down.

Yes No This person is your advocate and champions you with other leaders so that you gain others' respect even before you meet them.

EVALUATION

You can learn two things from this assessment: First, you can understand where you are with each person on the 5 Levels of Leadership based on your answers. If you answered *no* more times than *yes* in a section, then you have not gotten to that level with that person. (Instead, you would be on the level below that one.)

The second thing you can learn is where you need to work to improve. A *no* answer to any statement indicates where you need to do some work.

Part 3 — Leadership Assessment — Team Member's Point of View

Ask each of the people who report directly to you to fill out the following worksheet for you. They may do so anonymously if they wish. Use the same criteria for evaluating this assessment as you used to evaluate the Part 2 assessment you completed.

Note that even if you are a very good leader, you may have an employee or volunteer who refuses to put you anywhere but Level 1. You can try to win over that person on Level 2 and then progress, but there are no guarantees that the person will allow him- or herself to be won over.

LEADERSHIP ASSESSMENT

Name of Leader: **Date:**

_____ _____

Please read each statement and respond with yes or no in reference to the leader whose name is listed above. There are no right or wrong answers. This assessment is designed only to describe your interaction with the person. (If you wish, you may answer this assessment anonymously.)

Level 1

Yes   No   You acknowledge this person as your leader.

Yes   No   This person is well-suited for the leadership position he or she holds.

Yes   No   This person treats the leadership position as an opportunity to earn a place at the leadership table, not as a privilege to be used for personal advancement.

Level 2

Yes   No   This leader cares about your family and personal life outside of work and regularly asks you questions about them.

Yes   No   This leader knows your strengths and weaknesses.

Yes   No   This leader knows and respects your hopes and dreams.

Yes   No   This leader is committed to helping you succeed in your work.

Yes   No   You trust this leader and he or she trusts you.

Level 3

Yes   No   You respect this leader's professional ability and qualities.

Yes   No   You rely on his or her advice and expertise.

Yes   No   You have become more productive because of this leader's influence.

Yes   No   The team you are part of is more productive because of his or her leadership.

Yes   No   You and the team you are part of contribute to the vision and purpose of the organization.

Level 4

Yes   No   You have received specific training from this leader that has helped you to perform better.

Yes   No   This leader has mentored or developed you to help you become a better leader.

Yes   No   You are currently leading others as a result of opportunities and training given to you by this leader.

Yes   No   You believe in this leader and automatically give him or her the benefit of the doubt.

Level 5

Yes   No   You are training and developing other leaders thanks to the input from and influence of this leader.

Yes   No   You could step into your leader's role with a very high probability of success because he or she has helped to prepare you for it.

Yes   No   This leader has changed your life, and you are an advocate who champions him or her with other leaders.

Once you have completed the assessment, please return this document to the leader listed at the top of the page.

Part 4—Current Leadership Level Assessment

	Part 1 ＃ True	Part 2 ＃ On Each Level	Part 3 ＃ On Each Level	Predominant Level
Level 1				
Level 2				
Level 3				
Level 4				
Level 5				

You can gain a "snapshot" of your leadership by doing the following:

1. In the column labeled Part 1, record the number of statements you agreed with as true in each section of the assessment.
2. In the column labeled Part 2, record the number of your team members who are on each level with you based on your assessment of them.
3. In the column labeled Part 3, record the number of people who put you on each level according to their answers to the statements.
4. Now add the lines across. Which level of leadership has the highest number? More than likely, the one with the highest number indicates your current level of leadership with the majority of

people on your team. (This isn't meant to be scientifically valid. It's simply a tool to give you insight into yourself.)

Keep this assessment in mind as you move through the book. The Guide for Growth at the end of each section of the book will help you to improve your leadership skills and move up to the higher levels of leadership with your people.

Level 1:
POSITION

It's a Great Place to Visit,
But You Wouldn't Want to Live There

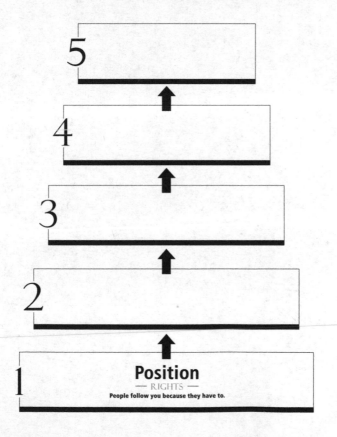

Leadership traditionally begins with Position. Someone joins the Army, and he or she becomes a recruit, working to earn the rank of private. A person gets a job, and along with it usually comes a title or job description: laborer, salesperson, waiter, clerk, accountant, manager. Position is the starting place for every level of leadership. It is the bottom floor and the foundation upon which leadership must be built. Real influence must be developed upon that foundation.

There was a time when people relied heavily on position to lead, which is no surprise when you consider that at one time, hereditary leadership positions were handed down from father to son (and sometimes daughter) within families. Princes became kings and their decisions were law — for good or bad. In most industrialized nations, those days are gone. True, there are still nations with kings and queens, but even in most of those nations, such as England, monarchs rule with the permission of the people, and the real leaders are usually elected. Position gives you a chance, but it usually carries with it very little real power, except in systems where the penalties for not following are dire.

There's nothing wrong with having a *position* of leadership. When a person receives a leadership position, it's usually because someone in authority saw talent and potential in that person. And with that title and position come some rights and a degree of authority to lead others.

Position is a good starting place. And like every level of leadership, it has its upside and downside. Let's start by looking at the good things about the Position level of leadership.

The Upside of Position

You Have Been Invited to the Leadership Table

Just as there are positive and negative aspects in every season of life, there are both positive and negative aspects to every level of leadership. If you are new to leadership and you receive a position, then there are things to celebrate. I'm going to tell you about four of them.

1. A Leadership Position Is Usually Given to People Because They Have Leadership Potential

Most of the time when people enter a leadership position, they do so because it was granted or appointed by some other person in authority. That probably seems obvious. But think about the implications: it usually means that the person in authority believes the new leader has some degree of potential for leading. That's good news. So if you're new to leadership and you have been invited to lead something, then celebrate the fact that someone in authority believes in you.

I remember the first time I was given a leadership position. I was named by my high school basketball coach to be the captain of our team. What an exhilarating moment that was! When I close my eyes, I can still remember how it felt to know that Coach Neff had confidence in me.

After he made the announcement, he shared with the other players that I was an example of positive attitude and hard work. But later he took me aside and explained that the title of captain would merely give me a platform to display my leadership abilities. It did not guarantee that the players would follow me. He said earning that would be my responsibility.

The best leaders promote people into leadership based on leadership potential, not on politics, seniority, credentials, or convenience.

> The best leaders promote people into leadership based on leadership potential, not on politics, seniority, credentials, or convenience.

John Wooden, the legendary UCLA basketball coach who was a fantastic leader, once told me that he didn't designate a captain for his team until after a few games into the season. He waited because he wanted to see which player would step up and deserve the honor. He has often been quoted as saying to his team, "Don't tell me what you're going to do, show me what you're going to do!"

If you have a new leadership position, then let me say welcome to the first step in your leadership journey. You have a seat at the table and have been invited to be part of the "leadership game." You will have opportunities to express your opinion and make decisions. Your initial goal should be to show your leader and your team that you deserve the position you have received.

2. A Leadership Position Means Authority Is Recognized

When an individual receives a position and title, some level of authority or power usually comes with them. Often in the beginning that power is very limited, but that's okay because most leaders need to prove themselves with little before being given much.

Going back to my first official leadership position—captain on the basketball team—I received certain new privileges. Before tip-off, I got to meet at center court with the referees and the other tain to discuss the game to be played. I could call time-ou game and was asked for input from the coach when we were in the huddle. I also spoke to the team in the locker room before and after each game. My title gave me recognition and authority. However, I also recognized the limitations of that recognition and authority. As the *Infantryman's Journal* (1954) says, "No man is a leader until his appointment is ratified in the minds and the hearts of his men."

As a new leader, you must use the authority you are given wisely, to advance the team and help the people you lead. Do that, and your people will begin to give you even greater authority. When that happens, you gain leadership, not just a position.

3. A Leadership Position Is an Invitation to Grow as a Leader

There should always be a relationship between receiving a leadership position and fulfilling the requirements demanded by it. One of the main requirements is personal growth. I learned this early in my life from my father, who loved to quote, "To whoever much is given, much shall be required." He believed that each of us had received a lot in life, and we had a responsibility to learn and grow so that we could make the most of it.

The journey through the 5 Levels of Leadership will only be successful if you dedicate yourself to continual development. If you believe that the position makes the leader, you will have a hard time becoming a good leader. You will be tempted to stop and "graze," meaning you'll stay where you are and enjoy the position's benefits, instead of striving to grow and become the best leader you can.

Frequently I'll ask a group, "What's the *one* thing you would change to improve the effectiveness of your organization?" Usually people name things that can be found on this list of Ps: products, promotions, policies, processes, procedures, pricing, and people. Seldom does anyone say the most important and impacting of all answers: "ME! I would change me to improve our organization." Yet that seldom-heard response is the key to success. If you want to lead, you need to grow. The only way to improve an organization is to grow and improve the leaders. If you want to make an impact, start with yourself.

The leaders who do the greatest harm to an organization are the ones who think they have arrived. Once they receive the title or position they desire, they stop growing. They stop innovating. They stop improving. They rest on their entitlements and clog up everything. Make the most of this opportunity in leadership by making growth your goal. And strive to keep growing. Good leaders are always good learners. To be an effective leader, you must believe that the leadership position you receive is merely an invitation to grow. If you do that and become a lifetime learner, you will continually increase your influence over time. And you will make the most of your leadership potential, no matter how great or small it might be.

4. A Leadership Position Allows Potential Leaders to Shape and Define Their Leadership

The greatest upside potential for people invited to take a leadership position is that it affords them the opportunity to decide what kind of leader they want to be. The position they receive may be defined, but they are not.

When you first become a leader, your leadership page is blank and you get to fill it in any way you want! What kind of leader do you want to be? Don't just become reactive and develop a style by default. Really think about it. Do you want to be a tyrant or a team builder? Do you want to come down on people or lift them up? Do you want to give orders or ask questions? You can develop whatever style you want as long as it is consistent with who you are.

Frances Hesselbein, founding president and chairman of the board of governors of the Leader to Leader Institute, observed, "Leadership is much less about what you *do*, and much more about who you *are*. If you view leadership as a bag of manipulative tricks or charismatic behaviors to advance your own personal interest, then people have

> "Leadership is much less about what you *do*, and much more about who you *are*."
> —*Frances Hesselbein*

every right to be cynical. But if your leadership flows first and foremost from inner character and integrity of ambition, then you can justly ask people to lend themselves to your organization and its mission."

If you are new to leadership—or new to a particular leadership position—it is the perfect time to think about the leadership style you desire to develop. (If you are an experienced leader, you can of course reevaluate the way you lead and make changes. However, you will be working against your people's past experiences and have to overcome their expectations.) As you move forward, what should you consider? Three things:

Who Am I?

Good leadership begins with leaders knowing who they are. In his book *It's Your Ship*, Capt. Mike Abrashoff states,

In a nutshell, hard experience has taught me that real leadership is about understanding yourself first, then using that to create a superb organization. Leaders must free their subordinates to fulfill their talents to the utmost. However, most obstacles that limit people's potential are set in motion by the leader and are rooted in his or her own fears, ego needs, and unproductive habits. When leaders explore deep within their thoughts and feelings in order to understand themselves, a transformation can take shape.[1]

Successful leaders work hard to know themselves. They know their own strengths and weaknesses. They understand their temperament. They know what personal experience serves them well. They know their work habits, their daily, monthly, and seasonal rhythms. They know which kinds of people they work well with and which kinds they have to try harder with to appreciate. They have a sense of where they are going and how they want to get there. As a result, they know what they're capable of doing and their leadership is steady.

Knowing yourself on a pretty deep level isn't quick or easy. It is a long and involved process. Some of it isn't particularly fun. But it is necessary if you want to become a better leader. Self-knowledge is foundational to effective leading.

What Are My Values?

In a speech on the value of honesty, Mark Twain once told this story: "When I was a boy, I was walking along a street and happened to spy a cart full of watermelons. I was fond of watermelon, so I sneaked quietly on the cart and snitched one. Then I ran into a nearby alley and sank my teeth into the melon. No sooner had I done so, however, than a strange feeling came over me. Without a moment's hesitation, I made my decision. I walked back to the cart, replaced the melon — and took a ripe one."

With all the problems we've witnessed in the banking industry, the implosion of Enron, and the failures of political leaders, I believe we understand what can happen when people treat their values like watermelons on the back of a cart, trading one for another. When leaders don't have and maintain strong core values, their actions impact many more people than just themselves.

> Your values are the soul of your leadership, and they drive your behavior.

Your values are the soul of your leadership, and they drive your behavior. Before you can grow and mature as a leader, you must have a clear understanding of your values and commit to living consistently with them—since they will shape your behavior and influence the way you lead.

As you reflect on your values, I believe you should settle what you believe in three key areas:

- **Ethical Values**—What does it mean to do the right thing for the right reason?
- **Relational Values**—How do you build an environment of trust and respect with others?
- **Success Values**—What goals are worth spending your life on?

If you answer these questions and commit yourself to living your values in these three areas, you'll be well on your way to developing the integrity that makes you attractive to team members and makes them want to follow your leadership.

Not long ago I came across a survey by Opinion Research Corporation for Ajilon Finance that confirms this. American workers were asked to select the one trait that was most important to them in a leader. While important to some, the majority of responders didn't identify expertise, competence, or even fairness as most important. Here are the results of the survey:

RANK	CHARACTERISTIC	PERCENTAGE
1	Leading by Example	26%
2	Strong Ethics or Morals	19%
3	Knowledge of the Business	17%
4	Fairness	14%
5	Overall Intelligence and Competence	13%
6	Recognition of Employees	10%[2]

Clearly, if leaders have a strong set of ethical values and live them out, then people will respect them, not just their position.

Immature leaders try to use their position to drive high performance. Mature leaders with self-knowledge realize that consistently high performance from their people isn't prompted by position, power, or rules. It is encouraged by values that are real and genuine.

What Leadership Practices Do I Want to Put into Place?

Herb Kelleher, the former chairman and CEO of Southwest Airlines, began his career as an attorney. In those early years, he learned some important lessons about leadership. He says:

My best lesson on leadership came during my early days as a trial lawyer. Wanting to learn from the best, I went to see two of the most renowned litigators in San Antonio try cases. One sat there and never objected to anything, but was very gentle with witnesses and established a rapport with the jury. The other was an aggressive, thundering hell-raiser. And both seemed to win every case. That's when I realized there are many different paths, not one right path. That's true of leadership as well. People with different personalities, different approaches, different values succeed not because one set of values or practices is superior, but because their values and practices are *genuine*.

If you want to become a better leader, you must not only know yourself and define your values. You must also live them out.

As you think about the way you will define your leadership, take into consideration what kinds of habits and systems you will consistently practice. What will you do to organize yourself? What will you do every day when you arrive at work? What spiritual practices will you maintain to keep yourself on track? How will you treat people? What will be your work ethic? What kind of example will you set?

Everything is up for grabs. It's up to you to define it. And the earlier you are on the leadership journey, the greater the potential for gain if you start developing good habits now.[3]

The bottom line is that an invitation to lead people is an invitation to make a difference. Good leadership changes individual lives. It forms teams. It builds organizations. It impacts communities. It has the potential to impact the world. But never forget that position is only the starting point.

The Downside of Position

True Leadership Isn't about Position

Like everything else in life, the Position level of leadership has negatives as well as positives. Each of the levels of leadership possesses downsides as well as upsides. You will find as you move up the levels that the upsides increase and the downsides decrease. Since Position is the lowest level of leadership, it has a great number of negatives. On Level 1, I see eight major downsides:

1. Having a Leadership Position Is Often Misleading

The easiest way to define leadership is by position. Once you have a position or title, people will identify you with it. However, positions and titles are very misleading. A position always promises more than it can deliver.

I learned this lesson about Level 1 when I received my first leadership position in my first church. I mistakenly thought that being named the pastor meant that I was the leader. I couldn't have been more mistaken, as I found out in my first board meeting. Soon after I officially started the meeting as the designated leader, the *real* leader took over. His name was Claude. He had lived in the rural valley where the church was located all his life, and everybody loved him. His influence was obvious as the other members of the board looked to him for direction and asked him questions regarding every issue. I could have

left the meeting and no one would have cared. In fact, I c
the meeting and no one would have noticed!

I was shocked. In that first meeting and all the subsequent ones, all eyes and attention were focused on Claude, the *real* leader. The board members were not following me, even though I had the job title, the calling, the appropriate college degree, the office, the salary—all of the positional "stuff." Claude had none of those things and yet they listened to everything he said.

My mistake was thinking that I had become a leader because of my position, instead of recognizing it as an opportunity to become a leader. I didn't understand that leadership was given to me but not yet earned by me. I was a little too much like the driver in this comic[4]:

LAUGH PARADE ®

BY BUNNY HOEST AND JOHN REINER

"This doesn't *really* make you leader material, Murray."

Back then I defined *leading* as a noun—as who I was—not a verb—as what I was doing. Leadership is action, not position. When I arrived at that first church, Claude had been earning his leadership influence through many positive actions over many years. And people followed him as a result. Claude, who was a down-to-earth farmer, explained it to me later, saying, "John, all the letters before or after a name are like the tail on a pig. It has nothing to do with the quality of the bacon."

> Leadership is action, not position.

I have come to embrace leadership as action, and I endeavor to teach that concept to leaders in conferences and seminars at home and abroad. One of the ways I do that is through my international nonprofit leadership organization, EQUIP, which has trained more than 5 million leaders in 160 countries. The organization's trainers and I have found the number one challenge in developing countries is introducing the idea of leadership as action instead of position. Leaders in these countries often possess an "I've arrived" mindset. We want them to understand one of the most important characteristics of leadership: leaders are always taking people somewhere. They aren't static. If there is no journey, there is no leadership.

> Leaders are always taking people somewhere. They aren't static. If there is no journey, there is no leadership.

2. Leaders Who Rely on Position to Lead Often Devalue People

People who rely on position for their leadership almost always place a very high value on holding on to their position—often above everything else they do. Their position is more important to them than the work they do, the value they add to their subordinates, or their contribution to the organization. This kind of attitude does nothing to promote good relationships with people. In fact, positional leaders often see subordinates as an annoyance, as interchangeable cogs in the organizational machine, or even as troublesome obstacles to their goal of getting a promotion to their next position. As a result, departments, teams, or organizations that have positional leaders suffer terrible morale.

Often to make themselves look better or to keep people from rising up and threatening them, positional leaders make other people feel small. How?

By not having a genuine belief in them.
By assuming people *can't* instead of assuming they *can*.
By assuming people *won't* rather than believing they *will*.
By seeing their *problems* more readily than their *potential*.
By viewing them as *liabilities* instead of *assets*.

Leaders who rely on their title or position to influence others just do not seem to work well with people. Some don't even *like* people! Why? It's a chicken-or-egg question, really. Do they not work well with people and as a result they rely on position? Or is it that because they rely on their position, they never take the time and effort to work well with people? I don't know. Maybe both kinds of positional leaders exist. But here's what I do know: They neglect many of the human aspects of leading others. They ignore the fact that all people have hopes, dreams, desires, and goals of their own. They don't recognize that as leaders they must bring together their vision and the aspirations of their people in a way that benefits everyone. In short, they do not lead well because they fail to acknowledge and take into account that leadership—of any kind, in any location, for any purpose—is about working with people.

3. Positional Leaders Feed on Politics

When leaders value position over the ability to influence others, the environment of the organization usually becomes very political. There is a lot of maneuvering. Positional leaders focus on control instead of contribution. They work to gain titles. They do what they can to get the largest staff and the biggest budget they can—not for the sake of the organization's mission, but for the sake of expanding and defending their turf. And when a positional leader is able to do this, it often incites others to do the same because they worry that others' gains will be their loss. Not only does it create a vicious cycle of gamesmanship, posturing, and maneuvering, but it also creates departmental rivalries and silos.

> Positional leaders focus on control instead of contribution.

For a very short time as a young leader I worked in a highly political environment like the one I described. It was like working in a minefield. There were many unwritten rules and hidden protocols for setting up appointments with superiors or selecting who you ate with at lunch. There was great emphasis placed on using proper titles to address people. And much of how you were treated depended on your background. Needless to say, I did not do well in that environment. I immediately looked for a better place to develop my leadership skills. When I found it and left, I was so happy. And so were they!

I have yet to find a highly political organization that runs at top efficiency and possesses high morale. Just look at most of our government institutions and think about the leaders and workers in them. Most people could certainly use improvement, and moving away from positional leadership would do a lot to help them.

4. Positional Leaders Place Rights over Responsibilities

One of my all-time favorite TV characters is Barney Fife, the deputy in the little town of Mayberry on *The Andy Griffith Show*. Don Knotts played Barney, and along with Andy Griffith, who played Sheriff Andy Taylor, he gave America one of its most successful TV series. I have watched every episode, some many times.

Barney Fife was your typical positional leader. His desire to feel important and have authority created many humorous story lines. Armed with one bullet and a badge, he took every opportunity to let people know he was in charge. He had rights as a lawman, and he wanted people to acknowledge them. Unfortunately for him (but fortunately for us in the audience), no one else took him seriously. The result was comic chaos, which seemed to follow him everywhere he went.

In contrast, Sheriff Andy, who seemed to spend all of his time being a calming influence on his misguided deputy, had the real authority and power. But he rarely used his position to get things done. He didn't carry a gun, either. Everyone knew he was the real leader and could handle any situation. Andy's focus was on his responsibility to the people he served, not on demanding respect or receiving the rights due to him because of his position. *The Andy Griffith Show* was lighthearted fun, but it was also a study in leadership.

Poet T. S. Eliot asserted, "Half of the harm that is done in this world is due to people who want to feel important.... They don't mean to do harm.... They are absorbed in the endless struggle to think well of themselves." That's what positional leaders do: they do things to make themselves look and feel important.

> "Half of the harm that is done in this world is due to people who want to feel important.... They do not mean to do harm.... They are absorbed in the endless struggle to think well of themselves."
> —*T. S. Eliot*

Inevitably, positional leaders who rely on their rights develop a sense of entitlement. They expect their people to serve them, rather than looking for ways to serve their people. Their job description is more important to them than job development. They value territory over teamwork. As a result, they usually emphasize rules and regulations that are to their advantage, and they ignore relationships. This does nothing to promote teamwork and create a positive working environment.

Just because you have the right to do something as a leader doesn't mean that it is the right thing to do. Changing your focus from rights to responsibilities is often a sign of maturity in a leader. Many of us were excited in early leadership years by the authority we had and what we could do with it. That power can be exhilarating, if not downright intoxicating. It's the reason President Abraham Lincoln said, "Nearly all men can stand adversity, but if you want to test a man's character, give him power." Each of us as leaders must strive to grow up and grow into a leadership role without relying on our rights. If we can mature in that way, we will start to change our focus from enjoying authority for its own sake to using authority to serve others.

> Just because you have the right to do something as a leader doesn't mean that it is the right thing to do.

5. Positional Leadership Is Often Lonely

The phrase "it's lonely at the top" must have been uttered by a positional leader—either that or by someone with a personality disorder! Leadership doesn't have to be lonely. People make it that way.

Positional leaders can become lonely if they misunderstand the functions and purpose of leadership. Being a good leader doesn't mean trying to be king of the hill and standing above (and set apart from) others. Good leadership is about walking beside people and helping them to climb up the hill with you. If you're atop the hill alone, you may get lonely. If you have others alongside you, it's hard to be that way.

> If you have others alongside you, it's hard to be lonely.

King-of-the-hill leaders create a negative work environment because they are insecure and easily threatened. Whenever they see people with potential starting to climb, it worries them. They fear that their place on top is being threatened. As a result, they under-mine the people who show talent, trying to guard their position and keep themselves clearly above and ahead of anyone else. What is the usual result? The best people, feeling undermined and put down, leave the department or organization and look for another hill to climb. Only average or unmotivated people stay. And they know their place is at the bottom. That develops an us-versus-them culture, with the posi-tional leader standing alone on top. Leadership doesn't have to be lonely. People who feel lonely have created a situation that makes them feel that way.

6. Leaders Who Remain Positional Get Branded and Stranded

As I began to lead people early in my career, I learned a valuable les-son. I always tried to set up new leaders for success, and I often gave them everything I could to help them become established leaders. A leadership position. My time. My influence. Modeling. Resources. Leadership opportunities. And here's what I found: if I gave the good potential leaders little or nothing, they still succeeded and became good leaders. In contrast, when I gave mediocre leaders everything I had, they still didn't succeed and couldn't establish themselves as good leaders. The position does not make the leader—the leader makes the position.

Whenever people use their position to lead others for a long time and fail to develop genuine influence, they become branded as posi-tional leaders, and they rarely get further opportunities for advance-ment in that organization. They may move laterally, but they rarely move up.

If you have been a positional leader, you can change, and this book will help you. However, you need to recognize that the longer you have relied on your position, the more difficult it will be for you to change others' perception about your leadership style. You may even need to change positions in order to restart the process of developing influence with others.

7. Turnover Is High for Positional Leaders

When people rely on their positions for leadership, the result is almost always high turnover. One of the chapters in my book *Leadership Gold* is titled, "People Quit People, Not Companies." In it I explain how people often take a job because they want to be part of a particular company, but when they quit it's almost always because they want to get away from particular people. Good leaders leave an organization when they have to follow bad leaders. Good workers leave an organization when the work environment is poor.

> People quit people, not companies.

Interview a person who has left and the odds are high that they did not leave their job. They left the people they had to work with.[5]

Every company has turnover. It is inevitable. The question every leader must ask is, "Who is leaving?" Are the 8s, 9s, and 10s leaving? Or the 1s, 2s, and 3s? If 8s are leaving and 3s are coming in, there's trouble ahead. Organizations with Level 1 leadership tend to lose their best people and attract average or below-average people. The more Level 1 leaders an organization has, the more the door swings out with high-level people and in with low-level ones.

About a year ago, my friend Linda Sasser wrote me a note in which she talked about the dynamics that occur when higher-level employees find themselves working for a positional leader. She says that these people often become Lost Leaders. Here's what Linda wrote:

It seems that a Level 1 leader also finds it difficult to h
3 employees. Good mid-level leaders make incompe
ers uncomfortable! So while it is true that employees will leave
a weak Level 1 leader, it is also true that Level 1 leaders will
remove Level 3 followers. Seeing this happen before my eyes
has fascinated me and of course saddened me.

So why do I call them lost leaders? They are great up-and-
comers who have been called to lead because of talent yet are
suppressed or driven away by Level 1 bosses, therefore leaving
them unemployed and lost amongst all the displaced workers.

What a waste of time and talent. Every time a productive worker or
potential leader is driven away by a positional leader, the organization
suffers. It's a fact that an organization will not function on a level
higher than its leader. It just doesn't happen. If a Level 1 leader is in
charge, the organization will eventually be a Level 1 organization.
If the leader is on Level 4, then the organization will never get to
Level 5 — unless the leader grows to that level.

8. Positional Leaders Receive People's Least, Not Their Best

Can you name one organization that gets the least from its people and
is the best at what it does? Can you name one coach who gets the least
from team members and has won a championship? Can you name one
teacher who gets the least from students yet ranks highest among
peers? Can you name one country that gets the least from its citizens
and is respected by the world? Can you name one marriage that gets
the least from each spouse that yields a great long-term relationship?
No, I bet you can't. Why? Because it is impossible to be successful
with people who give the least.

People who rely on their positions and titles are the weakest of all leaders. They give their least. They expect their position to do the hard work for them in leadership. As a result, their people also give their least. Some people who work for a positional leader may start out strong, ambitious, innovative, and motivated, but they rarely stay that way. Typically they become one of three types of people:

Clock Watchers

Followers who thrive in Level 1 leadership environments love clocks and they want them visible at all times throughout the building. Why? Because every moment at work is evaluated according to the clock. Before noon, whenever they look at the time, they think in terms of how long they've been there. "I've been here two hours." After lunch, it's how much time they have left. "Only two more hours until I go home." The clock also makes them aware of the more important times of the day: break time and lunchtime.

In Level 1 leadership environments, the morale of the employees begins to pick up after the afternoon break because it begins the countdown to the highlight of their day: quitting time. Around 4:30, the energy in the place really begins to increase. People are moving about the office putting things away. They clear their desks so that nothing can hinder them from leaving work at exactly 5:00 p.m.

At 4:45 they are walking around visiting and saying their good-byes to fellow employees. After all, they wouldn't want to seem rude by not saying good-bye when they go flying out of the door.

At 4:50 they go to the restroom one last time, no matter how much of their day they may have spent there. They wouldn't want to waste valuable personal time in the bathroom when they can do it on company time.

At 4:55 they replace their work shoes for track shoes. This ensures a quick getaway.

At 4:58 they get into starting position and wait for the clock to sound.

At 5:00 p.m. everyone is gone. Their exits have been coordinated, practiced, and timed to perfection.

At 5:02, not a single car is left in the parking lot, each one having been carefully backed into place that morning, ready for a quick escape.

Okay, so maybe I'm exaggerating just a bit. But that description is not that far from the truth. Clock watchers always know how much time is left before they get to go home, and they never want to work a moment beyond quitting time. But think about it: when the people who work with you can hardly wait to quit working with you, something is not working!

> When the people who work with you can hardly wait to quit working with you, something is not working.

Just-Enough Employees

Because positional leaders at Level 1 rely on their rights to lead and use their leadership position as leverage, the people who work for them often rely on their rights as employees and use the limits of their job descriptions as leverage to do only what's required of them. If they do that often and long enough, they can become just-enough people. They do just enough—to get by, to get paid, and to keep their job. For them, the big question is not, "What can I do to be a valuable employee?" Instead they ask, "How much must I do to be an employee?" They don't ask, "How can I advance and get promoted?" They only ask, "How can I keep from getting fired?"

When people follow a leader because they have to, they will do only what they have to. People don't give their best to leaders they like least. They give reluctant compliance, not commitment. They may give their hands but certainly not their heads or hearts. They are like the character in the cartoon here by Randy Glasbergen.[6]

Just-enough people have a hard time

> People don't give their best to leaders they like least.

**"I always give 110% to my job.
40% on Monday, 30% on Tuesday, 20% on
Wednesday, 15% on Thursday, and 5% on Friday."**

showing up. The only commitment they show is to taking off the maximum days allowed for any reason. Some spend a lot of mental energy finding creative ways of eliminating work. If only they used that commitment in positive ways!

The Mentally Absent

In a Level 1 environment, there are always individuals who may be physically present but mentally absent. They do not engage mentally and show up merely to collect a paycheck. This attitude is highly damaging to an organization because it seems to spread. When one person checks out mentally and doesn't receive any consequences for it, others often follow them. Mental turnover and sloppiness are contagious.

Evidently being mentally disengaged is also pretty common. The Gallup organization has tracked it for years and seen it bounce between 15 and 20 percent in the United States in recent years. In 2006, Gallup published a survey in the *Gallup Management Journal* showing stats through the second quarter of 2006. At that time they found that among workers eighteen or older in the United States, 15 percent (about 20.6 million people) were actively disengaged. Gallup estimated that it cost employers $328 billion.[7] And in a more recent survey, Gallup found that more than half of all German employees were disengaged from their work.[8]

Clarence Francis, former chairman of General Foods, said, "You can buy a man's time; you can buy his physical presence at a given place; you can even buy a measured number of his skilled muscular motions per hour. But you cannot buy enthusiasm...you cannot buy loyalty... you cannot buy the devotion of hearts, minds, or souls. You must earn these." People who rely on their position at Level 1 rarely earn more than "just enough" from their people. And that means they cannot achieve any great level of success, because accomplishment requires more than that. Success demands more than most people are willing to offer, but not more than they are capable of giving. The thing that often makes the difference is good leadership. That is not found on Level 1.

> Success demands more than most people are willing to offer, but not more than they are capable of giving. The thing that often makes the difference is good leadership.

When the people who work for a team, a department, or an organization give little of themselves, the results are mediocre at best. And morale is abysmal. Dick Vermeil, former Super Bowl–winning coach, remarked, "If you don't invest very much, then defeat doesn't hurt very much and winning is not very exciting." That is a pretty good description of a Level 1 leadership environment.

The greatest downside about Level 1 leadership is that it is neither creative nor innovative. It's leadership that just gets by. And if a leader stays on the *downside* of Level 1 long enough, he may find himself on the *outside*. If a leader fails on Level 1, there's nowhere to go but U-Haul territory. He'll be moving out and looking for another job.

Best Behaviors on Level 1

How to Make the Most of Your Position

If you have been leading on Level 1 and relying on your position or title to keep things going, are you destined to stay there forever? Absolutely not! All leaders can learn to lead differently and move up the levels of leadership if they're willing to change the way they lead on Level 1. How do you make the most of your leadership position while shifting from positional to permissional leadership? By doing three things:

1. Stop Relying on Position to Push People

There is nothing wrong with having a leadership position. That's the starting place for most leadership. However, there is everything wrong with having a positional mind-set. To become an effective leader on Level 1, you must stop relying on Position to push people.

The best leaders don't use their position at all to get things done. They use other skills. To help new leaders learn this lesson, Linda Sasser sometimes asks potential leaders to start leading *before* receiving a leadership position, just so she can see how they respond and to prepare them to move up the levels of leadership. She described it this way:

When I have a person whom I feel is ready to lead, I assign them a challenge that involves sacrifice, courage, and humbleness. I need to make sure before a title is given that this person experiences what it is like to be a leader. The choice to lead needs to be theirs and I need them to see that it is not always as glamorous as it appears. So I give them responsibility without the title and I do not tell others that this person will be leading them. The new leader has to figure out how to improve the performance of his or her teammates without having a title or positional authority.

At first it is very difficult for them. They often come back to me with frustrations, asking, "How can I tell them what to do when they don't have to follow me?" This creates perfect teaching moments. It allows me to question their approach. I say, "Why are you telling them what to do? A leader finds ways to influence action. Have you asked them how you can help them? Ask them about the challenges they have in their position. Maybe there is a way you can work together as a team and make things more efficient for one another. Form a relationship with this person and show interest in them."

Over time it is so exhilarating to see this process take place. What amazes me is what happens *after* I give these new leaders their title. Their teammates whom they were leading are usually thrilled when the person receives a leadership position. And their attitude of excitement is felt throughout the department. All this happens because the new leader has begun to learn that leadership isn't about the title or having an office. It's about influence and the fact that you can make an impact on others.

It's easy to fall back on position to push people, though it isn't always effective. Christian Herter, formerly the governor of Massachusetts, learned that the hard way when he was running for a second term of office. One day after a busy morning of campaigning without any time to stop for lunch, Herter arrived at a church barbecue. He was famished. As he moved down the serving line, he held out his plate to the woman serving chicken. She put one piece on his plate and turned to the next person in line.

"Excuse me," Governor Herter said. "You mind if I have another piece of chicken?"

"Sorry," said the woman. "I'm only supposed to give one piece of chicken to each person."

"But I'm starved," the governor said.

"Sorry, only one to a customer," said the woman.

The governor was a modest man, but he was also hungry, so he decided to throw a little weight around. "Lady, do you know who I am?" he said. "I am the governor of this state."

"Do you know who I am?" the woman said. "I'm the lady in charge of the chicken. Now, move along, mister!"

Nobody likes to be bossed around or to have someone else pull rank. Most people respond very poorly to positional leadership. How do you know if you possess a positional approach to leadership? Review the following concepts, which represent a positional mind-set. Level 1 leaders think:

Top-down — "I'm over you."

Separation — "Don't let people get close to you."

Image — "Fake it till you make it."

Strength — "Never let 'em see you sweat."

Selfishness — "You're here to help me."

Power — "I determine your future."

Intimidation — "Do this or else!"

Rules — "The manual says . . ."

In contrast, higher-level leaders think differently. The following captures how Level 2 leaders think:

Side by Side—"Let's work together."

Initiation—"I'll come to you."

Inclusion—"What do you think?"

Cooperation—"Together we can win."

Servanthood—"I'm here to help you."

Development—"I want to add value to you."

Encouragement—"I believe you can do this!"

Innovation—"Let's think outside the box."

Level 2 relies on people skills, not power, to get things done. It treats the individuals being led as people, not mere subordinates.

Whistler's Law says, "You never know who's right, but you always know who is in charge." Well, I think Whistler must have known some Level 1 leaders. The truth is that if you have to tell people that you're the leader, you're not. If you continue to rely on your position to move people, you may never develop influence with them, and your success will always be limited. If you want to become a better leader, let go of control and start fostering cooperation. Good leaders stop bossing people around and start encouraging them. That is the secret to being a people-oriented leader, because much of leadership is encouragement.

> "You never know who's right, but you always know who is in charge."
> —Whistler's Law

2. Trade Entitlement for Movement

Political philosopher Niccolò Machiavelli wrote, "It is not the titles that honor men, but men that honor titles." He understood the nature of leadership and the true weakness of titles. If you want to make the most of your position at Level 1 and to honor whatever titles you possess, then do not rely on them to lead others. Don't exercise your rights. Don't become possessive about your perks. And never believe that you deserve your position. Leadership isn't a right. It's a privilege. It must be continually earned. If you possess any sense of entitlement, that will work against you.

If you followed the presidential primaries in 2008, you may have noticed two telling examples of how a sense of entitlement can impact leadership. On the Republican side, Rudy Giuliani was the early favorite in the polls and many people believed he would receive the nomination of his party. He must have made a similar assumption, because when the primaries began, he decided not to enter the first few. Instead, he waited until the primary held in Florida. That state had a lot of delegates and he thought he would win it easily, then use that momentum to carry him forward and take the nomination for president. What happened? John McCain, who political experts gave little chance of winning the nomination, worked hard from the beginning and picked up a couple of wins, and the momentum began to shift. By the time the Florida primary came into play, the country was moving toward John McCain and away from Rudy Giuliani. Giuliani's sense of entitlement probably lost him the nomination.

On the Democratic side, Hillary Clinton was the early favorite in the polls and many people believed she would receive the nomination of her party. Unlike Giuliani, she worked hard from the beginning. However, she seemed to assume that she would have the nomination sewn up by Super Tuesday and didn't seem to have a strategy beyond that date. Meanwhile, Barack Obama waged his disciplined campaign, gained incredible momentum, and received the nomination. The rest, as they say, is history.

Good leaders don't take anything for granted. They keep working and keep leading. They understand that leadership must be earned and established. They remain dissatisfied in a way, because dissatisfaction is a good one-word definition for motivation. Good leaders strive to keep the people and the organization moving forward toward its vision. They recognize that organizations can sometimes be filled with appointments, but teams can be built only by good leadership.

You may have been appointed to a Level 1 position, but you will have to lead yourself and others above it. You must be willing to give up what is in order to reach for what could be. Let a vision for making a difference lift you and your people above the confines of job descriptions and petty rules. Forget about your leadership rights. Focus on your responsibility to make a difference in the lives of the people you lead. When you receive a position or title, you haven't arrived. It's time to start moving—and taking others along with you.

3. Leave Your Position and Move toward Your People

People who rely on position often mistakenly believe that it is the responsibility of the people to come to them for what they need and want. Good leaders understand that it is *their* responsibility to move toward their people. Leaders are initiators.

Greek philosopher Socrates said, "Let him that would move the world, first move himself." If you want to move up to Level 2 in your leadership, you need to get out of your territory. You need to stop being king of the hill, get down from your high place, and find your people. You must move beyond your job description, both in terms of the work you do and the way you interact with your people. You must make it your responsibility to learn who they are, find out what they need, and help them and the team win.

> "Let him that would move the world, first move himself."
> —*Socrates*

In order to do anything new in life, we must be willing to leave our comfort zone. That involves taking risks, which can be frightening. However, each time we leave our comfort zone and conquer new territory, it not only expands our comfort zone but also enlarges us. If you want to grow as a leader, be prepared to be uncomfortable. But know this: the risks are well worth the rewards.

The Laws of Leadership at the Position Level

People frequently want to know how the many concepts in my various books go together. As I've taught the 5 Levels of Leadership over the years, the book they've asked most about is *The 21 Irrefutable Laws of Leadership*. "Which laws do you practice on Level 1?" people ask. The truth is that every law can be practiced on every level. However, it is also true that certain laws are best learned as a person grows and moves up the 5 Levels of Leadership. I've included an explanation of the Laws of Leadership that best apply to each level. They are certainly not necessary for one to learn the 5 Levels, but they are provided for reference in the event that it can serve you in your growth process.

The Law of the Lid
Leadership Ability Determines a Person's Level of Effectiveness

Every person has a lid on his or her leadership potential. We are not all gifted equally. The challenge we all face is growing and developing to our full leadership potential, thereby raising the lid on our actual leadership ability.

The single greatest hindrance to a leader's growth is becoming positional in thinking. Anytime you think you've arrived — whether your position is the lowest or the highest in the organization — you've lowered your expectations for yourself, sold your leadership short, and fallen into a no-growth mind-set. People cannot reach their leadership potential by staying on Level 1.

If you are willing to forget about title and position, and instead focus on your potential, you will remove a great weight that would otherwise hold you down. If you want to break through your leadership lids and lift your leadership, you must move beyond Level 1.

The Law of Process
Leadership Develops Daily, Not in a Day

A leadership position can be received in a day, but leadership development is a lifelong process. Those who have a Position mind-set often say things like "Today I became a leader." What they need to think is, *Today I received a leadership position. I will endeavor every day to become a better leader.* That is embracing the Law of Process. Making that kind of statement emphasizes that the leadership appointment is only a starting point, and staying there means you would never actually begin your leadership journey.

The Law of the Navigation
Anyone Can Steer the Ship, But It Takes a Leader to Chart the Course

When you receive a leadership position, it's wise to recognize how early you are in the leadership journey and how much you still have to learn. The Law of Navigation is a good reminder of that.

My friend Bill Hybels loves to sail and is quite an accomplished sailor. A few years ago, he and I and our wives enjoyed a few days sailing in the British Virgin Islands along with two other couples. The boat we rented came with its own captain and crew, but we also got to participate in the sailing of the vessel. On the first day out, Bill had me at the wheel and he gave me instructions as I attempted to sail the boat. It wasn't easy, but after a few hours I began to get the hang of it.

Why do I mention this? Because as a novice sailor, I was able to steer the boat, but I certainly could not chart the course. It took an experienced leader to do that. Bill could have done it, but in our case, the boat's captain did.

If you are on Level 1 as a leader, know your limitations. You can learn to chart the course, but to do that you must move up to higher levels of leadership.

Beliefs That Help a Leader Move Up to Level 2

To change from a Level 1 leader to a Level 2 leader, you must first change the way you think about leadership. No one has to remain a positional leader, though the longer you have relied on your position, the longer it may take you to change the way you lead and the way others see you. You will have to earn your way up from Level 1.

Here are four statements you must embrace internally before you will be able to change from a positional leader to a permissional one:

1. Titles Are Not Enough

We live in a culture that values titles. We admire and respect people with titles such as doctor, CEO, chairman, PhD, Academy Award winner, director, Nobel Prize winner, salesman of the year, president, poet laureate. But what do those titles actually mean? Very little. The titles are ultimately empty, and you must learn to see them that way. People who make it their career goals to gain certain titles are not setting themselves up to be the best leaders they can be.

Who the person is and the work he does is what really matters. If the work is significant and adds value to people, then it doesn't need to come with a title. Many times we don't even have any control over whether we receive a title or an award. And for every person who has received recognition, there are thousands of others working without recognition who perhaps deserve even greater honor. Yet they continue to work without credit because the work itself and the positive impact on others are reward enough.

Developing an awareness that titles have little real value and that Position is the lowest level of leadership brings a healthy sense of dissatisfaction with Level 1 as well as a desire to grow. A Position is not a worthy destination for any person's life. Security does not give purpose. Leadership is meant to be active and dynamic. Its purpose is to create positive change.

> A Position is not a worthy destination for any person's life.

2. People—Not Position—Are a Leader's Most Valuable Asset

If you want to become a better leader, you can't focus on rules and procedures to get things done or keep things going. You must develop relationships. Why? Because the reality is that *people* get things done, not the playbook they use. And because people are the power behind any organization, they are its most valuable—and appreciable— asset.

Learning this lesson made a huge difference in my leadership life. During the first few years of my career, I was a Level 1 leader. I focused way too much on position and became position-driven. I was constantly wondering, *What are my rights? Is my authority clear? Where am I on the organizational chart? How do I compare to other leaders? How can I climb the ladder? Who do I need to know? What's the next step in my career path?* My preoccupation with position created frustration within me; if your focus is on position, you're never satisfied if you're not at the top. (Ironically, if you're focused on position and you do get to the top, you won't be satisfied with that either.)

I'm sorry to say that back then I was willing to use people to improve my position instead of using my position to improve people. That wasn't right. And it didn't work. When I finally realized that relying on Position and bossing over people wasn't the best way to get the best out of people, my attitude and actions started to change. I began to put people ahead of position. Instead of powering down, I started peopling up. Immediately, people noticed that my attitude had changed toward them.

It took some time to develop the people skills I needed to become a better leader, but it took no time at all to let others know that I valued them, expressing appreciation for them and taking interest in them personally. So that's a change you can make quickly, too. And here's the immediate benefit: The moment people noticed the shift in my attitude, I noticed a positive shift in their response to me. They began to help me, which allowed me to help them.

3. A Leader Doesn't Need to Have All the Answers

Positional leaders often believe that they need to have all the answers. After all, if they admit that they don't know something, it shows weakness. And if they show weakness, how are they going to stay on top of the hill and maintain their precious position? To get off of Level 1, a leader has to think differently.

When I started my career right out of college, I naïvely thought I had all the answers. Within a few months I realized I didn't, but I was afraid to admit it. My insecurity and immaturity caused me to act like Mr. Answer Man. It didn't matter how far outside of my expertise the question was. For a few years, I tried the "fake it 'til you make it" approach to leadership. However, I didn't fake it well, and others could tell. And, of course, that kind of approach doesn't help you to actually make it!

I began to realize that a leader's job is not to know everything but to attract people who know things that he or she does not. Once I recognized that one of us is not as smart as all of us, I stopped bringing people together to give them the answers and started calling on them

> One of us is not as smart as all of us.

to help me find the answers. That transformed my leadership, not only because I could be myself and stop pretending that I knew more than I did, but also because it harnessed the power of shared thinking.

4. A Good Leader Always Includes Others

Because positional leaders often work alone, standing atop the hill of leadership while their subordinates work together at the bottom, their teams work far under their capabilities. Why? Stand-alone leadership doesn't lead to teamwork, creativity, collaboration, or high achievement. What a shame, and what a waste of potential.

My father's generation possessed a lot of lonely leaders whose motto was "My way or the highway." As a result, they missed out on a lot. Moving up in the 5 Levels of Leadership is all about others. It means relating well to other people. It requires leaders to be examples for other people. It challenges them to develop and equip people. The higher you go up the levels of leadership, the more you realize that good leadership is about leading *with* others, not just leading others. It requires collaboration. It requires inclusion. It requires sacrifice of selfish personal ambition for the sake of the team and the vision of the organization. It means being part of something greater than yourself. It means putting others ahead of yourself and being willing to go only as fast as the people you lead.

A friend told me that when a group of Marines go into combat, they don't wear their insignia of rank. One reason is that they don't want officers and noncommissioned officers to be targeted by the enemy. But there's also another reason — when Marines go into battle, they know who's in charge. The chain of command has already been clearly established. Nobody needs a reminder of it. But not wearing symbols of rank also sends a clear message from leaders to followers: we are all in this together. We live or die together, regardless of rank.

Moving up from Level 1 to Level 2 requires the greatest personal change from a leader. It requires a change of beliefs and attitudes toward other people and leadership. But here's the truth: once you decide to include others in the leadership journey, you are well on your way to achieving success at the other levels.

Guide to Growing through Level 1

As you reflect on the upsides, downsides, beliefs, and best behaviors of the Position level of leadership, use the following guidelines to help you plan your growth.

1. **Thank the People Who Invited You into Leadership:** If you've ever been asked to take a leadership position, it's an indication that someone believed in you. Whether you were invited to lead a week or a decade ago, it's never too late to express gratitude to the person who invited you to the leadership table. Take the time to write a note or an e-mail to thank that person and express the positive impact leading has had on your life.

2. **Dedicate Yourself to Leadership Growth:** You will not grow as a leader unless you commit to getting out of your comfort zone and trying to be a better leader than you are today. Write a declaration of commitment to growth that describes what you will do to grow and how you will approach it. Then sign and date it. Put it someplace where you can reference it in the future. This marks the day you committed to becoming the leader you have the potential to be and to working your way up the 5 Levels of Leadership.

3. **Define Your Leadership:** Level 1 is the best place time defining your leadership and deciding what shape you want it to take. Use the three questions contained in the Level 1 section of the book to describe the kind of leader you desire to be:

- Who am I?
- What are my values?
- What leadership practices do I want to put into place?

4. **Shift from Position to Potential:** In the past, how have you expressed your career goals? Have you thought in terms of destinations, such as specific positions and titles, or have you thought in terms of the journey, meaning the work you will do while trying to achieve the greater vision? If you've thought in terms of position, change your focus. Instead, think about your leadership potential. What kind of leader do you have the potential to become? What kind of positive effect can you have on the people you lead? What kind of impact can you make on the world? Rewrite your goals to embrace a non-positional mind-set. It will make a difference in your teachability and the way you treat your team members.

5. **Focus on the Vision:** One of the ways to reduce an emphasis on title or position is to focus more on the vision of the organization and to think of yourself more as someone who helps clear the way for your people to fulfill that vision. To help you do that, take some time to rewrite your job description in those terms. Write down the vision of the organization and how your team or department helps to contribute to that vision. Then write down specific ways you can make it easier for your team members to do their part to fulfill the vision.

6. **Shift from Rules to Relationships:** If you have in the past relied on rules, regulations, and procedures to guide the people

you lead, then you need to make a shift to a more relational approach to leadership. Begin by looking for value in every person you lead. Then go out of your way to communicate how much you value each person. People are the most appreciable asset of any organization. You must be certain to treat them that way.

7. **Initiate Contact with Your Team Members:** If you have waited for people on your team to come to you for leadership, you need to change your approach to connecting with them. Get out of your office or cubicle and initiate contact with them. Make it your goal to get to know them, express your appreciation to them, encourage them, and offer your support to them.

8. **Don't Mention Your Title or Position:** If you are in the habit of pulling rank or reminding people about your title or position, commit yourself to stop doing those things. I would even recommend going as far as not mentioning your title anytime you introduce yourself. Do whatever you have to do to identify less with your title and position and more with how you contribute to the team or organization.

9. **Learn to Say, "I Don't Know":** If you have led thinking that you had to have all the answers, then change your approach to leadership. Good leaders don't have all the answers, but do enlist and empower people who will find the answers needed. Begin taking this approach immediately. For the next month, when someone asks for an answer that you don't know, admit it. Then ask for the opinions of the people on your team. If they don't have the answers to questions, ask them if they know people who do. Make problem solving collaborative.

10. **Find a Leadership Coach:** Most people find it very difficult to grow in leadership without the help of someone who's ahead of them in the journey. Think about the best leaders you know personally, and ask one of them to coach or mentor you. Ask if

you can meet with the person four to twelve times a year. Always prepare diligently before you meet by planning what questions you will ask and what problems you will ask for advice in solving. If you aren't prepared or don't have questions, don't ask for a meeting. Don't ever waste your mentor's time.

Level 2:
PERMISSION

You Can't Lead People Until You Like People

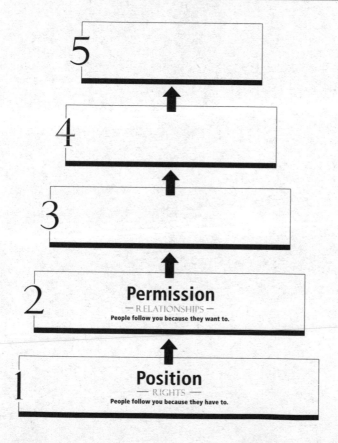

5

4

3

Permission
— RELATIONSHIPS —
People follow you because they want to.

2

Position
— RIGHTS —
People follow you because they have to.

1

Making the shift from Position to Permission brings a person's first real step into leadership. Why do I say that? Because leadership is influence, nothing more, nothing less. Leaders who rely on their positions to move people rarely develop influence with them. If their subordinates do what they are asked, it's usually because they think they *have* to — to receive their pay, keep their jobs, prevent being reprimanded, and so on.

In contrast, when a leader learns to function on the Permission level, everything changes. People do more than merely comply with orders. They actually start to follow. And they do so because they really *want* to. Why? Because the leader begins to influence people with *relationship*, not just position. Building relationships develops a foundation for effectively leading others. It also starts to break down organizational silos as people connect across the lines between their job descriptions or departments. The more barriers come down and relationships deepen, the broader the foundation for leading others becomes. When people feel liked, cared for, included, valued, and trusted, they begin to work together with their leader and each other. And that can change the entire working environment. The old saying is really true: people go along with leaders they get along with.

> **People go along with leaders they get along with.**

Relationships are a major key to success, whether you're trying to sell, coach, teach, lead, or simply navigate the daily tasks of life. In the context of sales, Jeffrey Gitomer, author of *The Sales Bible* and *Jeffrey Gitomer's Little Red Book of Selling*, uses the analogy of the rock-paper-scissors game to describe the importance of relationships.

Here's the rock, paper, scissors game of selling:
Relationship is more powerful than price.
Relationship is more powerful than delivery.
Relationship is more powerful than quality.
Relationship is more powerful than service.

That can also be said about leading. Relationships have great power.

Moving up to Level 2 is an important development in leadership because that is where followers give their supervisors *permission* to lead them. People change from being subordinates to followers for the first time, and that means there is movement! Remember, leadership always means that people are going somewhere. They aren't static. No journey, no leadership.

The Upside of Permission

The Workplace Has Become More Pleasant for Everyone

There are many upsides to Level 2 because the focus on relationship building opens up so many new avenues of leadership. Here are my top five:

1. Leadership Permission Makes Work More Enjoyable

Positional leaders often focus their efforts on serving themselves or their organization, with too little regard for others. However, leaders who move up to Level 2 shift their focus from *me* to *we*. They like people and treat them like individuals. They develop relationships and win people over with interaction instead of using the power of their position. That shift in attitude creates a positive shift in the working environment. The workplace becomes more friendly. People begin to like each other. Chemistry starts to develop on the team. People no longer possess a "have to" mind-set. Instead it turns to "want to." The workplace becomes more enjoyable for everyone—leaders and followers alike.

> Leaders who move up to Level 2 shift their focus from *me* to *we*.

The key to moving up to the Permission level is having the right attitude. Level 2 leaders exemplify the words of J. Donald Walters, who asserted, "Leadership is an opportunity to serve."

Permissional leaders like people and want to help them. They want to see them succeed. The prevalent attitude is one of serving others and bringing out the best in the people they work with.

I'm sorry to say that in my first professional leadership position, I focused way too much of my attention on myself and my organization. I knew where I wanted to go, and all I cared about in the beginning was getting there. What a mistake. It took me a couple of years to change my attitude and slow down enough to get to know people and find out what they cared about. It made a huge difference in my life and leadership. Now, more than forty years later, I have truly changed. Today my greatest joy comes from working with my team, not doing the work itself. I've gone from loving my work and looking for people to help me to loving my people and looking for ways to help them. As a result, the journey has become much more enjoyable.

2. Leadership Permission Increases the Energy Level

What happens when you spend time with people you don't especially like or who don't like you? Doesn't it drain you of energy? That kind of environment brings most people down. Even in a neutral environment, if you are with people you don't know very well, doesn't it require a lot of energy to get to know them? Connecting with others always takes energy. Conversely, what happens when you spend time with people you know and like? Doesn't it give you energy? I know it does me. Spending time with the people I love—whether at work, at home, or while playing—is my greatest joy, and it always energizes me.

Good relationships create energy, and they give people's interaction a positive tone. When you invest time and effort to get to know people and build good relationships, it actually pays off with greater energy once the relationships are built. And in that kind of positive, energetic environment, people are willing to give their best because they know the leader wants the best for them.

3. Leadership Permission Opens Up Channels
of Communication

On Level 2, top-down positional leadership is replaced with side-by-side relationships. That requires and cultivates good communication. On the Permission level, leaders listen to their people, and their people listen to them.

> On Level 2, top-down positional leadership is replaced with side-by-side relationships.

The interplay of communication between good leaders and their people on Level 2 can be found in a quote by former General Electric CEO Jack Welch. He describes an ideal leader as

somebody who can develop a vision of what he or she wants their business unit, their activity to do and be. Somebody who is able to articulate to the entire unit what the business is, and gain through a sharing of discussion—listening and talking— an acceptance of the vision. And [someone who] then can relentlessly drive implementation of that vision to a successful conclusion.[1]

Welch also commented, "Above all else, good leaders are open. They go up, down, and around their organizations to reach people. They don't stick to established channels. They're informal. They're straight with people. They make a religion out of being accessible."[2]

I believe most leaders are naturally better at talking than listening. I know that was true for me when I was early in my leadership journey. I was intent on communicating my vision to others and making sure they understood my agenda. I wanted communication to go only one way— from me to them. The result was that few people bought into my leadership or my vision. I failed to realize that the road to vision buy-in was a two-way communication. That meant I had to learn how to listen.

Recently I came across an explanation of the Chinese symbol for the verb "to listen." I thought it gave tremendous insight into the concept. The word, pronounced "ting," is made up of smaller symbols with specific meanings:[3]

Those symbols represent *you*, indicating that the focus is on the other person, not on yourself; the *ear*, the primary tool used in listening; the *eyes*, which we used to discover nonverbal clues to communication; *undivided attention*, which every person deserves if we intend to listen to all that is said; and the *heart*, which indicates that we are open to the other person on an emotional level, not just an intellectual one. In other words, when I really open up the channels of communication on Level 2 and really listen, here is what I must give others:

Ears — I hear what you say.
Eyes — I see what you say.
Heart — I feel what you say.
Undivided attention — I value who you are and what you say.

Only when we do these things are we able to build positive relationships and persuade people to follow us.

When leaders forge relationships on Level 2, they not only create better communication, they also build a community. Sociologist Amitai

Etzioni observed, "When the term *community* is used, the notion that typically comes to mind is a place in which people know and care for one another—the kind of place in which people do not merely ask 'How are you?' as a formality, but care about the answer." Level 2 leadership creates an environment where people begin to work together in a spirit of community and to communicate with one another openly.

4. Leadership Permission Focuses on the Value of Each Person

Level 2 leadership is relationally driven. That is only possible when people respect and value one another. It is impossible to relate well with those you don't respect. When respect lessens in a relationship, the relationship diminishes. You can care for people without leading them, but you cannot lead them effectively beyond Level 1 without caring for them.

> You can care for people without leading them, but you cannot lead them effectively beyond Level 1 without caring for them.

All great leaders value people. And they lift the value bar in their organizations. One of the greatest leaders in our lifetime is Nelson Mandela. He continually modeled a leadership that placed high value on every person. His strength and humility are legendary, and he was aware of how important his attitude was to his leadership. He observed, "You see, when there is danger, a good leader takes the front line. But when there is celebration, a good leader stays in the back room. If you want the cooperation of human beings around you, make them feel that they are important. And you do that by being humble."

Recently while on a trip to South Africa, I stopped in a bookstore in Johannesburg and picked up the book *Leading like Madiba: Leadership Lessons from Nelson Mandela*, by Martin Kalungu-Banda. I read it on my flight from South Africa to Kenya. It was filled with personal accounts of people who had witnessed their leader, Nelson Mandela, placing high value on people and lifting them up. One of my favorite stories was about a successful businessman named Peter, who had been invited by the president to come to his home and have breakfast.

On the day of their appointment, Peter dressed in his best and asked one of the company drivers, Dumi, to take him to Mr. Mandela's home. To Peter's amazement, his host was waiting for him in the parking area. Peter recalled,

I felt both extremely elated and humbled that Mr. Mandela was waiting outside for me. He warmly greeted the driver and me. He then gestured that we enter the house. However, in the traditional way of corporate behaviour and protocol, the driver retreated quietly and remained in the car. Mr. Mandela invited me to the breakfast table. Just before we started eating, my host seemed to miss something. He asked, "Peter, I thought there were two of you?" I responded, "No, sir. I came alone." "What about the other gentleman?" he insisted, and I replied, "No, sir. That one is just a driver. He will wait in the car." At that point Mr. Mandela stood up and went out to where the driver was. He introduced himself to the driver and asked him to join us for breakfast. Mr. Mandela then walked to the kitchen and said, "Dumi is joining us for breakfast. Can we have another plate, please?"[4]

Peter never forgot what Mandela did. And neither did Dumi. Peter went on to say, "When leaders learn to see the personalities that lie behind these seemingly humble titles [drivers, guards, and servants], the people in those jobs do not just feel appreciated, they discover and walk into new horizons of their lives. They become great performers at what they do. They find personal fulfillment." That is the impact great leaders can have on people. But you don't have to be a great leader to care about people. You just have to make the decision to do it!

Nothing lifts a person like being respected and valued by others. As a leader on Level 2, your goals should be to become aware of the uniqueness of people and learn to appreciate their differences. You need to let them know that they matter, that you see them as individual human beings, not just workers. This attitude makes a positive impact on people, and it strengthens your leadership.

At the beginning of my ministerial career, my father gave me a great piece of advice. He said, "Son, the vast majority of people who walk through the doors of the church feel undervalued, insecure, and lost. It's your job to change that." I never forgot that. And during my twenty-six-year career as a pastor, I always strove to follow that advice. I also try to bring it into my business relationships. I even do it at home. Every day I let my wife, Margaret, know how much I value her. When our children were growing up, we tried to provide an environment where we valued them and provided unconditional love. And as grandparents, Margaret and I enjoy seeing our grandchildren thrive as their parents and we show them every day how important they are to us.

There is a common thread in all great businesses, governments, educational centers, and religious institutions. That thread is everyone's valuing and respecting people. As a leader who moves up to Level 2, you can help to set an example of that for your organization.

5. Leadership Permission Nurtures Trust

Leaders who move up from Level 1 to Level 2 stop trying to impress others to maintain their position and start developing trust to maintain their relationships. That can be tough, because too often leaders place a higher value on impressing others than on having integrity with them. A story in a book by my friend Bill Hybels is a classic illustration of what can happen when leaders want others to be impressed. Bill writes,

A newly promoted colonel...had moved into a recently built makeshift office during the Gulf War. He had just arrived and was just getting things organized when out of the corner of his eye, he saw a private coming his way, carrying a tool box.

Wanting to seem important, he quickly spun around and picked up his phone. "Yes, General Schwarzkopf, yes, yes of course, I think that's an excellent plan," he said. "You've got my support on it. Thanks for checking with me. Let's touch base again soon, Norm. Goodbye." And he briskly hung up and turned around.

"And what can I do for you?" he asked the private.

"Ahh, I'm just here to hook up your phone."[5]

Trust is the foundation of Permission. If you have integrity with people, you develop trust. The more trust you develop, the stronger the relationship becomes. The better the relationship, the greater the potential for a leader to gain permission to lead. It's a building process that takes time, energy, and intentionality.

Retired admiral James Stockdale said, "When the crunch comes, people cling to those they know they can trust—those who are not detached, but involved." That is the power of Permission. In times of difficulty, relationships are a shelter. In times of opportunity, they are a launching pad. Trust is required for people to feel safe enough to create, share, question, attempt, and risk. Without it, leadership is weak and teamwork is impossible.

> "When the crunch comes, people cling to those they know they can trust—those who are not detached, but involved."
> —James Stockdale

The Downside of Permission

The Pressure Is on You to Build Positive Relationships

If you're a relational person, as I am, you may be saying to yourself, *What downside can there possibly be to developing relationships, building trust, and gaining people's permission to lead them? Isn't it all good?* My answer has to be no. While it is true that the positives far outweigh the negatives, there are still downsides to Level 2. Here are the ones I have observed:

1. Permission Leadership Appears Too Soft for Some People

In a hard-charging, high-performance, leadership-intensive environment, leading by Permission may appear "soft" to some people. Caring for people and being relational can be seen as weak, especially by leaders who possess a natural bias toward action (rather than affection). For that reason, some people dismiss it. What a mistake — and what a handicap to their leadership potential.

It's been my observation that most people start their leadership focused on either the "hard" aspects of leadership, meaning the productivity side, or on the "soft" aspects, meaning the relational side. Those who start on the hard side and refuse to learn softer skills often get stuck on Level 1. They desire to go to Level 3 Production, but they can't achieve it without learning and earning Level 2 first.

In contrast, those who start on the soft side gladly and easily work their way up to Level 2 Permission, but if they don't do more than just win relationships, they get stuck and never move up to Level 3 Production, either. It takes both Permission and Production to become a good leader.

I started my leadership career on the soft side. Here is the good news: I quickly built relationships with people. Here's the bad news: I never wanted to make hard decisions. I found it easy to love people, but when loving people created tension for leading them, I usually stopped leading. One of the reasons has to do with my upbringing. I grew up in a loving home, and as a result I mistakenly thought I could just love people to the top. But I also fell into the trap of wanting to make only decisions that were approved and accepted by all. I got stuck on Level 2 because my "softness" became a lid on my leadership.

It took an internal crisis to finally help me see what I was doing wrong. It occurred in my first pastorate, which was in a little country church in southern Indiana. Each year the congregation voted on whether to keep the pastor. As a young leader that first year in the church, my thoughts and actions had been dominated by making everyone happy. I had done everything in my power to do that, and I thought I had succeeded.

Then the vote came. For as long as I live, I will never forget the results: 31 yeses, 1 no, and 1 abstention. I was devastated! When your goal is to please *everyone*, and *anyone* is displeased, it is seen as a failure. I couldn't believe that someone didn't like me. And it was almost just as bad that someone else didn't even care one way or the other.

That night after everyone else had gone home, I called my father.

"Dad," I said, "I don't know what I should do. Should I stay or should I go?" I was shocked to hear him laughing on the other end of the line.

"Son, trust me, you need to stay," he responded. "It's the best vote you will ever have."

I stayed. But I still wasn't leading right. For the next few months I constantly asked myself two questions: Who voted against me? And what did I do wrong? My immaturity made me think that good leaders always had buy-in from everyone, they didn't have to deal with conflict, and they could avoid the reality of making hard decisions. (And, by the way, he was right. In my career, it was the best vote I ever had.)

I was stuck in this wrong kind of thinking for several months. But then I realized what my real problem was: I was a people pleaser. My goal had been to make everyone happy. That was the wrong goal. As a leader, my goal should have been to help people, not to make them happy.

That realization changed my leadership. For the first time I was freed up. I was no longer held captive by every person's opinion, which was a very unhealthy place to be. I could focus on doing what I believed was best for the organization and the people. Making everyone happy isn't responsible. Nor is it even possible. This realization made me more courageous and more realistic at the same time.

I needed to add the hard side of leadership to my natural bent toward the relational soft side. Others have to learn the soft side and add it to the hard, productive side. The point is you need both. If you're relational without being productive, you and your team won't achieve any progress. If you're productive without being relational, you may make a small degree of progress in the beginning, but you'll fall short in the long run because you'll either alienate your people or burn them out. You can't become successful in leadership until you learn both.

2. Leading by Permission Can Be Frustrating for Achievers

High achievers want to get things done and get them done *now*! They usually don't want to slow down for anything or anyone. Leading by permission requires them to do exactly that. Building relationships takes time. It can be very slow work.

If at one end of the spectrum you have achievers ignoring relationships, at the other end you have highly relational people who allow the relationships to become an end unto themselves. That's not healthy, either. In fact, the most common reason for leaders not moving up to Level 3 is that they become so relational that they lose sight of the primary goal of leadership: helping others work together, move forward, and achieve. When relationships become an end unto themselves, then high-achieving followers who focus on bottom-line results become restless. When that happens, they often try to do one of two things: take over or leave. You must win both levels as a leader to be successful.

If you're a high achiever who has neglected relationships in your leadership, you may be saying to yourself, *I haven't needed to develop relationships to be a good leader. I don't think a leader really needs Level 2.* Here is my answer to that: as long as you're winning, people are willing to follow — even if you are hard on them or positional in your leadership. However, when you drive people to achieve without slowing down to build relationships, a part of them will want to see

> If you step on people's fingers on the way up, they may trip you on the way down.

you lose. There's a saying that if you step on people's fingers on the way up, they may trip you on the way down. At the very least, if you fail, they'll celebrate your fall and then move on.

3. Permissional Leaders Can Be Taken Advantage Of

People whose leadership style is nonrelational are usually seen as no-nonsense leaders. Positional leaders often use their positions to distance themselves from subordinates. High achievers sometimes intimidate their followers. But when leaders are relational, their followers naturally get closer to them. That sometimes means that they mistake kindness for weakness. They believe that encouragement means they don't have to respect boundaries. They assume that empowerment means they have the freedom to do whatever they want. As a result, they take advantage of their leaders.

I have to admit this has happened to me. When I have encouraged people, some have built on it. Others have taken advantage of it. Developing close relationships with people who work with me has resulted in some lifelong friendships that I cherish deeply. But it has also resulted in some lifelong disappointments.

As you build relationships with people on Level 2, I believe you will find that there are four kinds of people:

- **Takers:** Those who leverage the relationship to better themselves, but not you or anyone else. They borrow your influence but keep the return.
- **Developers:** Those who leverage the relationship in a positive way, bettering themselves and you.
- **Acquaintances:** Those who live off of their relationship with you but never do anything with it. They hang around waiting for something good to come to them, content to live off of others' successes and never taking responsibility to grow themselves.
- **Friends:** Those who enjoy their relationship with you, returning your good will and never taking unfair advantage of it.

Being relational is a risk, just as it is when you open yourself up to falling in love. Sure, you can stay guarded and never get hurt. But you will also never have the chance to have deep, rewarding relationships that will enrich your life and the lives of others. I hope you will choose to build relationships. I made that choice early in my leadership life, and though I have been hurt and I've occasionally had others take advantage of me, I don't regret it. Most people respect the relationship, treat it the right way, and add great value to me.

4. Permission Leadership Requires Openness to Be Effective

Author and pastor Rick Warren observes, "You can impress people from a distance, but you must get close to influence them." When you do that, they can see your flaws. However, Warren notes, "The most essential quality for leadership is not perfection but credibility. People must be able to trust you."

> "The most essential quality for leadership is not perfection but credibility. People must be able to trust you."
> —*Rick Warren*

Most people don't want to admit their mistakes, expose their faults, and face up to their shortcomings. They don't want to be discovered. They don't get too close to people because of the negatives in their lives. And if people receive a leadership position, the urge to hide their weaknesses can become even stronger. Most people believe they must show greater strength as leaders. However, if leaders try to maintain a façade with the people they lead, they cannot build authentic relationships.

To develop authentic relationships on the Permission level, leaders need to be authentic. They must admit their mistakes. They must own up to their faults. They must recognize their shortcomings. In other words, they must be the real deal. That is a vulnerable place to be for a leader. And truthfully, it is one of the main reasons many leaders never progress from Level 1 to Level 2 in leadership.

5. Permission Leadership Is Difficult for People Who Are Not Naturally Likable

If we're honest, we must admit that some individuals are naturally gifted with people. They interact well with others and easily develop relationships. Level 2 comes naturally for such people. But what about people who are not naturally gifted at working with people? For them moving up to Level 2 usually doesn't come as easily. If they want to win Permission with others, they have to work to make themselves more likable.

For years I have observed people who do not work well with others, and I have asked myself why they don't. My conclusion is that in most cases, people who are not likable don't like people very much. I'm not saying that they *hate* others. But I am saying that they don't care for others enough to commit the energy needed to make good connections with them.

I believe that people will not get ahead with others unless they are willing to get behind others. How can we do that? How can we become more likable? By doing the following:

- Make a choice to care about others. Liking people and caring about people is a choice within your control. If you haven't already, make that choice.
- Look for something that is likable about every person you meet. It's there. Make it your job to find it.
- Discover what is likable about yourself and do whatever you can to share that with every person you meet.
- Make the effort every day to express what you like about every person in your life.

If you want to win people's permission and lead effectively on Level 2, you must like people and become more likable.

6. Permission Leadership Forces You to Deal With the Whole Person

Auto pioneer Henry Ford once asked, "Why is it that I always get the whole person when what I really want is a pair of hands?" Let's face it: relationships are messy. Many leaders would rather deal with people only in terms of their work life. But the reality is that when you lead someone, you always get the whole person—including their dysfunctions, home life, health issues, and quirks.

Good leaders understand that the heart of leadership is dealing with people and working with the good, the bad, and the ugly in everyone. They do this on Level 2. Leadership experts Warren Bennis and Burt Nanus put it this way:

> Leadership is an essentially human business. Both universities and corporations seriously miss the point with their overemphasis on formal quantitative tools, unambiguous problems, and ridiculously oversimplified "human relations" cases. What we have found is that the higher the rank, the more interpersonal and human the undertaking. Our top executives spend roughly 90 percent of their time concerned with the messiness of people problems.[6]

I think if we're honest, we have to admit that the messiness of people problems is what can make leadership no fun. So often, as we get to know others and we start to see their flaws, we become disillusioned with them. And we often end up like the woman at a cocktail party who was trying her best to look happy. Someone noticed a gargantuan sparkling rock on her finger and exclaimed, "Wow! What a beautiful diamond!"

"Yes," she said, "it's a Callahan diamond."

"I wish I had one!" the onlooker replied.

"No, you don't," the woman tartly responded.

"Why not?"

"Because it comes with the Callahan curse."

"The Callahan curse — what's that?"

With a deep sigh and a forlorn look, she said, "Mr. Callahan!"

The more we learn about others, the more disappointed we may be. Why? Because each of us has imperfections and irritating habits. We all fail. After the Nixon years, Billy Graham said, "Everybody has a little Watergate in him." We must learn to accept that about one another and still work together.

As a leader, you may be tempted to build relationships only with the people you like or with whom you are highly compatible, and to ignore the others. However, by doing that, you have the potential to lose a lot of people. It's important to remember that while the things we have in common may make relationships enjoyable, the differences are what really make them interesting. Good leaders on Level 2 deal successfully with these differences and leverage them for the benefit of the team and organization.

Good leaders are able to look at hard truths, see people's flaws, face reality, and do it in a spirit of grace and truth. They don't avoid problems; they solve them. Abolitionist leader Frederick Douglass once said that you can't expect to get a crop without plowing, and you can't expect rain without thunder and lightning. Leaders who build relationships understand that conflict is a part of progress. Often it is even constructive.

The bottom line on Level 2 is that most of the downsides of leadership come from dealing with people. If you care about people and understand them, then you expect things not to go smoothly. If you go into leadership on the Permission level with that expectation, it frees you to lead with a positive attitude and an open mind. You know that as long as people still have a pulse, you will be dealing with messy and difficult situations.

Best Behaviors on Level 2

How to Gain People's Permission

If you find yourself in a place where you need to start working to win people's permission on Level 2, what should you do? How can you make the most of the opportunity to develop as a relational leader? Do the following:

1. Connect with Yourself Before Trying to Connect with Others

One of the secrets of connecting with people and building relationships is knowing and liking yourself. In my book *Winning With People*, I call it the Mirror Principle, which says, "The first person we must examine is ourselves." The work in relationship building always has to start with yourself. What does that mean?

The First Person I Must Know Is Myself—Self-Awareness

Human nature seems to endow people with the ability to size up everybody in the world but themselves. Very few people are gifted with natural self-awareness. So what is a person to do? Become a student of yourself. Learn your strengths and weaknesses. Ask others to evaluate you. Understand the way you think, feel, and act in every kind of situation. Then once you know who you are, forget about yourself and place your focus on others. You will relate to other people from a place of strength.

The First Person I Must Get Along With Is Myself—Self-Image

I know people who've never gotten along with themselves a single day in their lives. They don't like how they look. Or they wish they had been endowed with different gifting or a different personality type. They don't like where they came from or where they're going. There are a lot of things you can change about yourself. Work hard at those. But there are also many you can't. Accept them. Take the advice of Thomas Jefferson: in matters of conscience, stand like a rock; in matters of fashion, go with the flow.

The First Person to Cause Me Problems Is Myself—Self-Honesty

Comedian Jack Paar quipped, "Looking back, my life seems like one big obstacle race, with me being the chief obstacle." Most people

> It's very difficult to be self-deluded and successful at the same time.

who don't get anywhere in life have themselves to blame. They don't believe in themselves. They create problems and then pretend they are someone else's fault. They want change but won't grow. It's very difficult to be self-deluded and successful at the same time. Even the few who manage to pull it off can never sustain it. If you want to build relationships, you need to be honest—starting with yourself.

The First Person I Must Change Is Myself—Self-Improvement

If you want to change your life for the better, then the first thing you must do is change yourself for the better. Author Samuel Johnson advised that "he who has so little knowledge of human nature as to seek happiness by changing anything but his own disposition will waste his life in fruitless efforts and multiply the grief which he purposes to remove." Too often we look outside of ourselves for the source of our problems. The reality is that many come from inside of us.

The First Person Who Can Make a Difference Is Myself—Self-Responsibility

Every significant accomplishment begins with one person stepping up and committing to make a difference. That person then takes responsibility to pass it on to others. If you don't take responsibility for yourself, then don't expect your life to become any different from what it is right now.

2. Develop a People-Oriented Leadership Style

Permissional leaders don't rely on rules to lead people. They don't depend on systems. And they never try to rule with a stick. (Anyone who does needs to know that every stick eventually breaks.) Instead, they use a personal touch whenever they deal with people. They listen, learn, and then lead. They develop relationships. They have more than an open-door policy—they know the door swings both ways. They go through it and get out among their people to connect.

Herb Kelleher said, "Leading an organization is as much about soul as it is about systems. Effective leadership finds its source in understanding. Unless a leader has an awareness of humanity, a sensitivity toward the hopes and aspirations of those he leads, and the capacity to analyze the emotional forces that motivate conduct, he will be unable to produce and be successful regardless of how often other incentives are given."

> "Leading an organization is as much about soul as it is about systems. Effective leadership finds its source in understanding."
> —Herb Kelleher

Another way to say it is that good leaders *never* take people out of the equation in anything they do. They always take people into account—where they are, what they believe, what they're feeling. Every question they ask is expressed in the context of people. Knowing what to do isn't enough to make someone a good leader. Just because something is right doesn't necessarily mean that people will let you do it. Good leaders take that into account. And they think and plan accordingly.

If you want to be successful on Level 2, you must think less in terms of systems and more in terms of people's emotions. You must think more in terms of human capacity and less in terms of regulations. You must think more in terms of buy-in and less in terms of procedures. In other words, you must think of people before you try to achieve progress. To do that as a permissional leader, you must exhibit a consistent mood, maintain an optimistic attitude, possess a listening ear, and present to others your authentic self.

3. Practice the Golden Rule

One of the criticisms of permissional leadership is that it can become manipulative. I agree that leaders who put an emphasis on motivating people can use leadership for personal gain at the expense of others. There is a fine line between manipulating people and motivating them. However, a permissional leader can keep that tendency in check and keep from crossing over from motivation to manipulation by following the golden rule.

I am often given the opportunity to travel internationally and speak to a wide variety of audiences with different cultures, languages, histories, values, and interests. However, all request that I spend some time teaching them about integrity in relationships. In those situations, I always teach the golden rule: "Treat others as you want others to treat you." That simple rule can be universally understood and followed. It establishes the relationship standard that make sense and can be applied. And it is a core teaching that can be found in every culture and religion. It is the simplest, most profound, and most positive guide to living there is. Take a look at how many variations on the golden rule I was able to find and the religions from which they come:

Christianity: "Whatever you want men to do to you, do also to them."[7]

Islam: "No one of you is a believer until he loves for his neighbor what he loves for himself."[8]

Judaism: "What is hateful to you, do not do to your fellow man. This is the entire Law; all the rest is commentary."[9]

Buddhism: "Hurt not others with that which pains yourself."[10]

Hinduism: "This is the sum of duty; do naught unto others what you would not have them do unto you."[11]

Zoroastrianism: "Whatever is disagreeable to yourself, do not do unto others."[12]

Confucianism: "What you do not want done to yourself, do not do to others."[13]

Baha'i: "And if thine eyes be turned towards justice, choose thou for thy neighbour that which thou choosest for thyself."[14]

Jainism: "A man should wander about treating all creatures as he himself would be treated."[15]

Yoruba Proverb (Nigeria):"One going to take a pointed stick to pinch a baby bird should first try it on himself to feel how it hurts."[16]

It is clear that the golden rule cuts across cultural and religious boundaries and is embraced by people from nearly every part of the world. And what does practicing the golden rule in leadership do? It enables everyone to feel respected. That changes the entire environment of a department or an organization. When leaders change from driving people in a positional environment to respecting people

> **Practicing the golden rule enables everyone to feel respected.**

in a permissional environment, their people go from feeling like a stake to feeling like a stakeholder.

4. Become the Chief Encourager of Your Team

For many years I have enjoyed the friendship of the Cathy family, the leaders of Chick-fil-A. One day when I was having dinner with Truett Cathy, the company's founder, he said, "Do you know how I identify someone who needs encouragement? If the person is breathing they need a pat on the back!"

I have yet to meet a person who doesn't enjoy and benefit from encouragement. No one is too successful, old, experienced, or educated to appreciate positive praise and encouragement from another person. A great example of this can be found in the lives of two talented authors and teachers: C. S. Lewis and J. R. R. Tolkien. The friends, both professors at Oxford, often met to share with each other the fiction they were writing. When Tolkien was writing *The Lord of the Rings*, he became discouraged. Lewis continually encouraged his friend to keep writing. "Tollers, where's the next chapter? You can't give up now," Lewis would chide. In later years, Tolkien acknowledged how much of a difference Lewis's positive input had made: "The unspeakable debt I owe him cannot be fathomed," wrote Tolkien. "For long, he was my only audience."

As a leader, you have great power to lift people up. Mother Teresa said, "Kind words can be short and easy to speak, but their echoes are endless." I'm sure Lewis's encouraging words echoed in Tolkien's ears as he labored to write his fantasy masterpiece. As a leader, you can have a similarly positive impact on others. People enjoy affirmation from a peer. But they really value it from their leader. The

> "Kind words can be short and easy to speak, but their echoes are endless."
> —*Mother Teresa*

words "I'm glad you work with me; you add incredible value to the team" mean a lot coming from someone who has the best interest of the team, department, or organization at heart.

If you want people to be positive and to always be glad when they see you coming, encourage them. If you become the chief encourager of the people on your team, they will work hard and strive to meet your positive expectations.

5. Strike a Balance between Care and Candor

Many people get the wrong idea about the concept of permissional leadership when they become acquainted with it. Some think that succeeding on the Permission level of leadership means treating the people on their team like family. That is almost always a mistake. People don't deal realistically with their family. I don't. I have a commitment level with them that is deeper than with others. Regardless of what they do, I am committed to giving them unconditional love. They have privileges that I extend to no other people. And compromise is a constant. (Anyone who says they don't believe in compromise has never been married—or stayed married.) What makes a family great isn't what makes a team great. Families value community over contribution. Businesses value contribution over community. The best teams strike a balance.

Others think being a permissional leader means giving team members permission to do whatever they want. That idea is also wrong. Just because you care about people doesn't mean you let them work without responsibility or accountability. If you care about people, treat them with respect, and build positive relationships with them, you actually have more numerous opportunities to speak candidly and have hard conversations with them that will help them to grow and perform better.

Every person has problems and makes mistakes in the workplace.

Every person needs to improve and needs someone to come alongside them to help them improve. As a leader, it is your responsibility and your privilege to be the person who helps them get better. That often begins with a candid conversation. But before you have it, it helps to ask yourself what the nature of the problem might be. My friend Sam Chand says that when he is having difficulty with a person he asks himself one simple question, "Is this person a *can't* or a *won't*? *Can't* is about abilities. We can help these kinds of people in most cases—not in all cases, but in most. But *won't* is about attitude. If the issue is attitude, the time to let that person know there is a problem is now, because here is the deal: we hire people for what they know and fire them for who they are."

I believe that people can change their attitudes and can improve their abilities. And because I do, I talk to them about where they're coming up short. If you're a leader and you want to help people, you need to be willing to have those tough conversations. So how does a leader handle being relational while still trying to move people forward? By balancing care and candor. Care without candor creates dysfunctional relationships. Candor without care creates distant relationships. But care balanced with candor creates developing relationships.

> Care without candor creates dysfunctional relationships. Candor without care creates distant relationships.

Allow me to help you understand how care and candor work together to help a leader succeed on Level 2:

Caring *Values the Person While* Candor *Values the Person's Potential*

To lead successfully on Levels 2 and higher, it is important for you to value people. That is foundational to solid relationships. Caring for others demonstrates that you value them. However, if you want to help them get better, you have to be honest about where they need to improve. That shows that you value the person's potential. That requires candor.

One of the secrets of being candid is to think, speak, and act in terms of who the person has the potential to become and to think about how you can help them to reach it. Proverbs says,

Faithful are the wounds of a friend,
But deceitful are the kisses of an enemy.[17]

If you're candid with others but with their benefit in mind, it doesn't have to be harmful. It can be similar to the work of a surgeon. It may hurt, but it is meant to help and it shouldn't harm. As a leader, you must be willing and able to do that. If not, you won't be able to help your people grow and change.

Caring *Establishes the Relationship While* Candor *Expands the Relationship*

The things that usually help to establish a relationship are common ground and care. But those things usually aren't enough to make a relationship grow. To expand a relationship, candor and open communication are required.

Most leaders I talk to have a difficult conversation that they know they need to have but are avoiding. Usually they are reluctant for one of two reasons: either they don't like confrontation, or they fear that they will hurt the person they need to talk to. But if a leader can balance care and candor, it will actually deepen and strengthen the relationship.

Let me give you an example. Sheryl came to work for me because she was a real go-getter with a lot of potential. For six months, I watched her work, and what I discovered was that she was great at the hard side of leadership. She was energetic. She was organized. She was a good planner. And she always got things done. But she totally neglected the soft side of leadership—the relational part. She wasn't winning over anyone she was leading. As a result, she wasn't gaining influence, which meant that her leadership was going to be very limited.

I scheduled a meeting with her so that we could have a candid conversation about her leadership style. I let her know how much I respected her ability and how much I cared about her as a person. But I also let her know where she was falling short and how that would limit her in her ability to lead people. I also offered to coach her on the relational side. To her credit, she accepted my criticism and took my help.

For the next couple of years, I met with her regularly, critiqued her interaction with others, gave her reading assignments, and asked her to do things that would stretch her. She blossomed as a leader and began to win people on Level 2. And that freed her to keep growing. It wasn't long before she worked her way up to Level 4 with many people in the organization.

Not everyone responds well to candid conversations. Let's face it: honesty can hurt. Some people shut down when you criticize them. Others leave and work somewhere else. However, if you have candid conversations with someone and that person hangs in there and grows, she will make herself a candidate for the climb up to Level 3 and beyond, just as Sheryl did.

Caring *Defines the Relationship While* Candor *Directs the Relationship*

Solid relationships are defined by how people care about one another. But just because people care about one another doesn't mean that they are going anywhere together. Getting the team moving together to accomplish a goal is the responsibility of the leader, and that often requires candor. My friend, Colin Sewell, owner of several auto dealerships, said to me, "Leaders have to make the best decisions for the largest group of people. Therefore, leaders give up the right to cater to an individual if it hurts the team or the organization."

Getting results always matters, and good leaders never lose track of that. One night at a bas-

> "Leaders have to make the best decisions for the largest group of people. Therefore, leaders give up the right to cater to an individual if it hurts the team or the organization."
> —Colin Sewell

ketball banquet the president of a junior college was congratulating the coach and the team profusely. The beaming coach asked the president, "Would you still like me as much if we didn't win?"

"I'd like you as much," the president replied. "I'd just miss having you around."

Retired army general and former secretary of state Colin Powell noted, "Good leadership involves responsibility to the welfare of the group, which means that some people will get angry at your actions and decisions. It's inevitable—if you're honorable." If you want to lead people well, you need to be willing to direct them candidly.

Caring *Should Never Suppress Candor, While* Candor *Should Never Displace Caring*

The bottom line, which has already become very clear, is that good leaders must embrace both care and candor. You can't ignore either. So to help you keep the balance between the two, I've created a caring candor checklist for working with people. Before having a candid conversation, make sure that you can answer yes to the following questions:

- Have I invested enough in the relationship to be candid with them?
- Do I truly value them as people?

- Am I sure this is their issue and not mine?
- Am I sure I'm not speaking up because I feel threatened?
- Is the issue more important than the relationship?
- Does this conversation clearly serve their interests and not just mine?
- Am I willing to invest time and energy to help them change?
- Am I willing to show them how to do something, not just say what's wrong?
- Am I willing and able to set clear, specific expectations?

If you can answer yes to all of these questions, then your motives are probably right and you have a good chance of being able to communicate effectively.

As a young leader, I found it very difficult to have candid conversations with people. I often postponed those difficult talks, hoping that an issue would go away. Seldom did that happen. Maybe you relate to that. If so, you'll be glad to hear that you're normal. However, you need to know that candid conversations are a leader's responsibility and must be done—but in the right way with the right attitude. When an employee is hired to get a certain job done and doesn't, that hurts the team and the organization. And then it's time for the leader to take action. That can be very hard; but in the long term, it's best not only for the organization but also for the person who needs to hear what's not going right.

The next time you find yourself in a place where you need to have a candid conversation, just remember this:

- Do it quickly—shovel the pile while it's small.
- Do it calmly, never in anger—use the caring candor checklist.
- Do it privately—you want to help the person, not embarrass him or her.
- Do it thoughtfully, in a way that minimizes embarrassment or intimidation.

If your goal is to help the individual, improve the team, and fulfill the vision of the organization, then this is the path you should follow as a leader.

As you work with people and have candid conversations, allow me to remind you of one more thing: candidness is a two-way street. If you want to be an effective leader and earn your way onto Level 2, you must allow the people you work with to be candid with you. You must solicit feedback. And you must be mature and secure enough to take in people's criticism without defensiveness and learn from it. Leadership expert Warren Bennis observed, "Effective leaders reward dissent, as well as encourage it. They understand that whatever momentary discomfort they experience as a result of being told from time to time that they are wrong is more than offset by the fact that 'reflective back talk' increases a leader's ability to make good decisions."[18] Caring for people, making good decisions for everyone involved, and building solid relationships is what Level 2 is all about. This is Permission at its best.

The Laws of Leadership at the Permission Level

I f you want to use the Laws of Leadership to help you grow and win Permission on Level 2, then consider the following:

The Law of the Influence
The True Measure of Leadership Is Influence— Nothing More, Nothing Less

If you boil leadership down to its essence, it is influence. Leaders help people work together to accomplish goals that benefit everyone involved. How does one person get others to do something willingly, excellently, and consistently? By influencing them.

When I first developed the 5 Levels, I called it The 5 Levels of Influence. Why? Because each time leaders climb a level, their influence increases. The influencing process begins at Level 2, where relationships are formed. That is where leadership begins the shift from coercion to cooperation.

The Law of Addition
Leaders Add Value by Serving Others

Why do people initially want to be in leadership? Is it to gain power? To have more freedom? To receive a bigger paycheck? To feed their ego? Many times leaders begin their careers with selfish motives. Maybe that's not a good thing. But it doesn't have to be a bad thing if we are willing to change and put our focus on others.

I've observed that most Level 1 leaders who have no desire to move up to Level 2 Permission haven't gotten beyond the selfishness of wanting a leadership position for their own benefit. To move up to Level 2, leaders need to understand that great leaders practice the Law of Addition. They lead in order to help people and add value to them.

The Law of Solid Ground
Trust Is the Foundation of Leadership

Trust is the foundation not only of leadership relationships but of all relationships. You cannot influence people who don't trust you. You cannot build positive relationships with people if they perceive you negatively. Trust is the glue that holds people together.

Trust begins at Level 2 and it grows as you climb to the higher levels of leadership. If people trust you, they will be willing to move upward with you. Without trust, you'll quickly find yourself back down at Level 1.

The Law of Magnetism
Who You Are Is Who You Attract

I've studied leadership dynamics since I was a teenager, and something I noticed early is that birds of a feather flock together. It is a fact of life that like-minded people are attracted to one another. Groups of people tend to be of similar age, values, and background. I've also seen that leaders attract who they are, not necessarily who they want.

As you gain influence in your department or organization, that can be good news or bad news. If the people who start flocking to you are relational, nonterritorial, teachable, and productive, then that is a positive statement about your leadership. If they are positional, close-minded, and unmotivated, then that reflects negatively on your leadership. If you want to change your team, then change yourself.

The Law of Connection
Leaders Touch a Heart Before They Ask for a Hand

If you want to build relationships and gain people's permission to lead them, then work hard to connect with them. I define *connecting* as having the ability to identify with and relate to people in such a way that it increases your influence with them. That is what you must do on Level 2 to win them over and earn the right to lead them.

> *Connecting* is having the ability to identify with and relate to people in such a way that it increases your influence with them.

The Law of Buy-In
People Buy into the Leader, Then the Vision

Leaders are by nature visionary. They have great hopes. They have big dreams. They want to win, and win big. But a great vision without a great team often turns into a nightmare. Teamwork makes the dream work. (I'll discuss how to build a team on Level 3.)

Often leaders share their visions with me and then ask, "Do you think my people will buy into my vision?" When they ask me this, I know they don't understand Level 2 Permission and probably haven't won it yet with their people. Why do I say that? Because they're asking the wrong question. Instead, they should be asking, "Have my people bought into me?"

The size or the worthiness of a leader's vision often isn't what determines whether it will be achieved. The determining factor is usu- ally the level of the leader. Before you ask people to move forward to achieve the vision, they must first buy into you as the leader. Before they buy into you as the leader, you must have earned their trust and gained permission to lead them. That begins on Level 2.

Beliefs That Help a Leader
Move Up to Level 3

Moving up to Level 2 from Level 1 is a significant advance in leadership ability. Very often an achiever or a producer will be given a leadership position at Level 1 with the expectation that the person can make the transition from worker to leader. Most of the people who fail to move up into leadership don't make it because they never understand the importance of building relationships with the people they work with and gaining their permission to lead them. However, there are still more leadership levels to be won.

If you have worked your way up to Level 2 with people and have gained their confidence as a person who cares about them, then it's time to start thinking the way a Level 3 leader does. To begin that shift, keep in mind the following three things:

1. Relationships Alone Are Not Enough

Although the Permission level may bring you and your team great satisfaction relationally, if you stay on Level 2 and never advance, you won't really prove yourself as a leader. The good news is that if you've connected with your team, you now have some influence with them. The question now is: what are you going to do with that influence?

True leadership takes people somewhere so that they can accomplish something. That requires a leader to connect people's potential to their performance. The Permission level is foundational to good leadership, but it is not your ultimate goal.

2. Building Relationships Requires Twofold Growth

Throughout this chapter I've written about building relationships. In doing that, I've focused on how people need to grow *toward* each other. But for relationships to be meaningful, there is another kind of growth that's also needed. People must also grow *with* each other. Growing toward each other requires compatibility. Growing with each other requires intentionality.

If you are married or in a significant long-term relationship, then you probably understand how these dynamics come into play. When you first met your partner, you moved toward one another, based on attraction, common ground, and shared experiences. You established the relationship. However, a relationship can't last if you never go beyond those initial experiences. To stay together, you need to sustain the relationship. That requires common growth. If you don't grow together, there's a very good chance you may grow apart.

Similarly, if you are to have any staying power as a leader, you must grow toward and with your people. Just because you've developed good relationships with your people, don't think that you're done on the relational side. There is still more work to do.

3. Achieving the Vision As a Team Is Worth Risking the Relationships

Building relationships with people can be hard work. But to succeed as a leader and to move up to the higher levels of leadership, you have to be willing to risk what you've developed relationally for the sake of the bigger picture. Leaders must be willing to sacrifice for the sake of the vision. If achieving the vision is worth building the team, it is also worth risking the relationships.

Building relationships and then risking them to advance the team creates tension for a leader. That tension will force you to make a choice: to shrink the vision or to stretch the people to reach it. If you want to do big things, you need to take people out of their comfort zones. They might fail. They might implode. They might relieve their own tension by fighting you or quitting. Risk always changes relationships. If you risk and win, then your people gain confidence. You have shared history that makes the relationship stronger. Trust increases. And the team is ready to take on even more difficult challenges. However, if you risk and fail, you lose relational credibility with your people and you will have to rebuild the relationships.

Risk is always present in leadership. Anytime you try to move forward, there is risk. Even if you're doing the right things, your risk isn't reduced. But there is no progress without risk, so you need to get used to it.

The bottom line is that you can slow down early in your leadership to build relationships on Level 2, or you can forge ahead trying to skip straight to Level 3—but if you do, you will have to backtrack later to build those relationships. And you need to recognize that doing that will slow your momentum, and it can actually take you longer to build the team than if you did it the right way in the first place.

Starbucks founder Howard Schultz said, "If people relate to the company they work for, if

> "If people relate to the company they work for, if they form an emotional tie to it and buy into its dreams, they will pour their heart into making it better."
> —Howard Schultz

they form an emotional tie to it and buy into its dreams, they will pour their heart into making it better." I believe that is true. What is the key link between people and the company? The leader they work with! That leader is the face, heart, and hands of the company on a day-to-day basis. If that leader connects and cares, that makes a huge difference.

Guide to Growing through Level 2

As you reflect on the upsides, downsides, best behaviors, and beliefs related to the Permission level of leadership, use the following guidelines to help you grow as a leader:

1. **Be Sure You Have the Right Attitude toward People:** The key issue when it comes to the Permission level of leadership is how much you like people and how much they like you. And here's the good news. You can control how much you like people, and in general, if you genuinely like people, they will find you to be likable. This may seem too simplistic, but make a decision to like everyone from today forward—even if they don't like you. Write out that intention, then sign and date it. If you need to, keep it in front of you as a daily reminder to make people a priority.

2. **Connect with Yourself:** To become someone who is good at building relationships with others, you must become the kind of person *you* would want to spend time with. Using the five components listed in the chapter for connecting with yourself, put yourself on a growth plan that will help you to win the following:

   Self-Awareness—know your personality type, temperament, talents, strengths, and weaknesses.

Self Image — deal with any personal issues you may have so that you can think of yourself in a positive way.

Self-Honesty — look at yourself realistically and decide to face reality, no matter how much it may hurt.

Self-Improvement — make a commitment to grow in your ability to develop relationships.

Self-Responsibility — acknowledge that you are responsible for your own actions and attitudes.

3. **Understand Where You're Coming From:** Are you a naturally relational person who tends to put people ahead of productivity? Or are you an achiever who tends to put productivity ahead of people? You must recognize which you are, and learn to win both relationships and results.

4. **Express Value for Each Person on Your Team:** Take some time and come up with positive things that you can honestly say about each person on your team. Then take the time during the next week to tell each person at least one positive thing about themselves.

5. **Evaluate Where You Are with Your Team:** Write a list with the names of the people on your team. Now for each, determine how well you know them by answering the following questions (which come from materials the Eli Lilly corporation developed from the 5 Levels of Leadership):

What three nonbusiness things do you know about this person?

What does this person value?

What are this person's top three concerns?

What does this person want or hope for in life?

If you are unable to answer these questions for someone on your team, then you need to spend more time getting to know that person. Set aside time this week to get to know him or her better.

6. **Accept the Whole Person As a Part of Leading:** If you want to be a good leader, you don't get to use people's time and skills while ignoring or neglecting the rest of them as individuals. That's not fair or right. Learn to accept responsibility for helping people and dealing with the messy side of leadership, or step down and get out of leading (without standing on the sidelines and criticizing the way other people lead).

7. **Make Fun a Goal:** One of the best ways for goal-oriented individuals to develop a more people-oriented style of leadership is to try to make the workplace more fun. If you're more task-oriented than people-oriented, then make fun a goal on your to-do list. That will make it more palatable for you while at the same time making you more likable.

8. **Give People Your Undivided Attention:** Many people in the workplace today feel dehumanized and demoralized. They believe that the leaders and organizations they work for don't care about them as people. To counter that, when you engage with people, pay attention and really listen. Few things communicate that you care for people better than giving them your undivided attention. And it doesn't cost you anything but time.

9. **Become Your Team's Encourager-in-Chief:** People are naturally attracted to people who give them confidence and make them feel good about themselves. You can be a leader who does that if you're willing to become an intentional encourager. Try it out. For the next two weeks, say something encouraging to someone on your team every day. Then watch to see how the person responds. Do that with everyone on your team, and they will not only want to work with you, but they will also get more done.

10. **Practice Care and Candor:** If you care about your people, you'll want to be honest with them in a way that helps them. When you see that someone on your team is making mistakes or in some way falling short, plan to talk with the person immediately. Use the caring candor checklist to make sure you do it in the right way. And remember, it's hard to go wrong as long as you're practicing the golden rule.

Level 3:
PRODUCTION

*Making Things Happen Separates
Real Leaders from Wannabes*

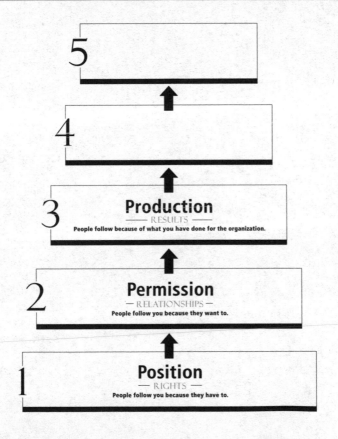

5

4

3 **Production**
— RESULTS —
People follow because of what you have done for the organization.

2 **Permission**
— RELATIONSHIPS —
People follow you because they want to.

1 **Position**
— RIGHTS —
People follow you because they have to.

The Production level is where leadership really takes off and shifts into another gear. Production quali-
fies and separates true leaders from
people who merely occupy leadership
positions. Good leaders always make
things happen. They get results. They
can make a significant impact on an

> Production qualifies and
> separates true leaders from
> people who merely occupy
> leadership positions.

organization. Not only are they productive individually, but they also
are able to help the team produce. This ability gives Level 3 leaders
confidence, credibility, and increased influence.

No one can fake Level 3. Either you're producing for the organization and adding to its bottom line (whatever that may be), or you're
not. Thomas Watson, the founder of IBM, noted, "The outstanding
leaders of every age are those who set up their own quotas and constantly exceed them." That is a good description of Level 3 leaders.
They are self-motivated and productive. As a result, they create
momentum and develop an environment of success, which makes the
team better and stronger.

Another benefit of leadership on Level 3 is that it attracts other
highly productive people. Producers are attractive to other producers.
They respect one another. They enjoy collaborating. They get things
done together. That ultimately creates growth for the organization.

Leaders can get to Level 1 for an almost endless number of reasons: They show promise. They have connections. They play politics.
They have seniority. The organization is desperate. You name it, and
someone has probably received a leadership position because of it.
Leaders who are naturally good with people or who take pains to learn
people skills can move up to Level 2. But some people never move up

from Level 2 Permission to Level 3 Production. Why? They can't seem to produce results. When that is the case, it's usually because they lack the self-discipline, work ethic, organization, or skills to be productive. However, if you desire to go to higher levels of leadership, you simply have to produce. There is no other way around it.

The Upside of Production

You Now Have Leadership Credibility

With the addition of Production, people's leadership really begins to hit its stride. Built on a foundation of strong relationships, leaders who get results dramatically improve their team and organization. There are so many upsides to Level 3. Here are six:

1. Leadership Production Gives Credibility to the Leader

The ability to produce results has always been the separation line for success. It is also the qualifying line for leadership. Peter Drucker, often described as the father of modern management, expressed it this way: "There are two types of people in the business community: those who produce results and those who give you reasons why they didn't."

> "There are two types of people in the business community: those who produce results and those who give you reasons why they didn't."
> —*Peter Drucker*

Authentic leaders know the way and show the way to productivity. Their leadership talk is supported by their walk. They deliver results. They live on their performance, not their potential. They lead by example. And their ability to get results tends to silence their critics and build their reputations.

Colin Powell asserted, "You can issue all the memos and give all the motivational speeches you want, but if the rest of the people in your organization don't see you putting forth your very best effort every single day, they won't either." Level 3 leaders *take* their people where they want them to go—they don't *send* them there. They are more like tour guides than travel agents. Why? Because people always believe what we do more than what we say. Therefore the credibility of a Level 3 leader can be summed up in one word: *example*.

> The credibility of a Level 3 leader can be summed up in one word: *example*.

Recently I ran across the story of a great general from history named Epaminondas. A leader of Thebes, he was a brilliant military tactician who defeated the vaunted Spartans. His victories brought him great acclaim, but they also produced enemies within his own city.

The opponents of Epaminondas could find no easy way to destroy or discredit him, so instead they sought to humiliate him. They put him in charge of collecting the city's garbage, a thankless job in a filthy city.

Even though he knew his appointment to the job was done out of spite and was meant to humiliate him, he accepted it with dignity, saying "If the position will not reflect glory on me, I will reflect glory on the work."[1]

I suspect that the story is apocryphal, but it still proves the point. If we do our work with excellence and help others to be productive, we gain great leadership credibility.

I found this to be true in my own career. As I was graduating from college with a bachelor's degree, two churches offered me the job of being their pastor. One was in Maysville, Kentucky. It offered an excellent salary and benefits and was an exceptional place to begin my ministry career. The other was in Hillham, Indiana. It was a very small church in the middle of nowhere that could not afford to pay me a full-time salary.

I chose Hillham over Maysville. Why? I wanted to prove to myself and others that I could lead people and build a congregation. My father advised me that Hillham would be a better place to learn. It was one of my best decisions as a leader.

During the three years that I led that church, it grew and prospered in many ways. Many people began to attend the church for the first time, people were growing spiritually, and we were recognized as the fastest-growing church in the denomination. We even had to buy land and build a new building.

It was in Hillham that I learned to move up from Level 1 Position, to Level 2 Permission, to Level 3 Production. My leadership credibility my peers was established there, and doors for greater opportunities quickly opened to me. Those are some of the reasons I say that every young leader should have a place like Hillham to learn how to lead.

Poet Walt Mason wrote a poem called "The Welcome Man," which describes the credibility that Level 3 leaders have. Here is an excerpt:

> *There is a man in the world who is never turned down,*
> > *wherever he chances to stray;*
> *He gets the glad hand in the populous town,*
> > *or out where the farmers make hay;*
> *He is greeted with pleasure on deserts of sand,*
> > *and deep in the isles of the woods;*
> *Wherever he goes there's the welcoming hand—*
> > *he's The Man Who Delivers the Goods.*[2]

People welcome achievers who deliver the goods—who get results.

2. Leadership Production Models and Sets the Standard for Others Visually

Producers and achievers always have an impact on the people who work with them and for them. To illustrate the point, I want to share my all-time favorite story, called "Sel not Spel":

A newly hired traveling salesman wrote his first sales report to the home office. It so stunned the brass in the sales department because it was obvious that the new sales person was ignorant! Here's what he wrote:

"I seen this outfit which they ain't never bot a dime's worth of nothing from us and I sole them some goods. I'm now goin to Chicawgo."

Before the man could be given the heave-ho by the sales manager, along came this letter from Chicago:

"I cum hear and sole them haff a millyon."

Fearful if he did, and afraid if he didn't fire the ignorant salesman, the sales manager dumped the problem in the lap of the president.

The following morning the ivory towered sales department members were amazed to see—posted on the bulletin board above the two letters written by the ignorant salesman—this memo from the president:

"We ben spending two much time trying to spel instead of tryin to sel. Let's watch those sails. I want everybody should read these letters from Gooch who is on the rode doin a grate job for us and you should go out and do like he done."[3]

Okay, I admit that it's a corny story, but I just love it because it shows how loudly productivity speaks in any organization. Gooch in the story may not be a Level 3 speller, but he is certainly a Level 3 producer. And as a result, the company president held up his example as the standard to follow.

That's how it is in leadership. Productivity puts people at the head of the class. And when that producer has already done the slower work of building relationships on Level 2, his or her leadership really takes off!

I had to learn this the hard way. When I came out of college, someone could have written a book about all the things I *didn't* know. I was just a kid and had no idea how little I knew. But I liked people and I worked hard. And I could produce. As a result, new worlds opened up to me very quickly. I was surprised and pleased when people started asking me to speak at conferences to tell my story. As a result, my influence began to grow, and soon leaders began to visit our church and ask more questions. Many times these leaders were older and much more experienced than I was. I found that very humbling. But it also inspired me to want to help people more. That was when I began to develop resources. I wanted to keep helping people long after my personal contact with them was finished. This eventually led to my writing books and being published.

I don't tell you this to brag. What I'm really trying to communicate is that *anyone* who can produce has a chance to influence people at a higher level. That's the power of Level 3 Production. If you can develop solid relationships with people and you can produce, you can be an effective leader.

Productive leaders are an example to the people they lead, and their productivity sets the standard for the team. President Abraham Lincoln recognized this. During the American Civil War, the president relieved General John C. Fremont of his command. He said it was for this reason: "His cardinal mistake is that he isolates himself and allows no one to see him." Lincoln knew that leaders need to be among their people, inspiring them with their ability, letting them see what the standard should be for their performance. When leaders produce, so do their people. Productive leaders thrive on results—from themselves and the team. They show the way and others follow.

3. Leadership Production Brings Clarity and Reality to the Vision

Good leaders constantly communicate the vision of the organization. They do it clearly, creatively, and continually. But that doesn't mean that everyone who receives the message understands and embraces it. The Production level of leadership communicates the vision through action, which helps people understand it in ways they may not have before. When followers see positive results and see goals being met, they get a clearer picture of what it means to fulfill the vision.

One day during the American Revolutionary War, George Washington rode up to a group of soldiers trying to raise a beam to a high position. The corporal who was overseeing the work kept shouting words of encouragement, but they couldn't manage to do it. After watching their lack of success, Washington asked the corporal why he didn't join in and help.

The corporal replied quickly, "Do you realize that I am the corporal?"

Washington very politely replied, "I beg your pardon, Mr. Corporal, I did."

Washington dismounted his horse and went to work with the soldiers until the beam was put into place. Wiping the perspiration from his face, he said, "If you should need help again, call on Washington, your commander in chief, and I will come."

Level 3 leaders help their people to see what productivity looks like. And with each day of productivity, the team gets one step closer to making the vision a reality. That encourages members of the team.

It validates their efforts. It makes the vision that much clearer. And clarity is compelling. Productivity also expands the vision, because with increased confidence and skill, the people doing the work recognize that they can actually accomplish more than they may have believed was possible.

4. Leadership Production Solves a Multitude of Problems

Many people in leadership positions try to solve problems by using systems. Or they pay others to try to solve problems for them. But the truth is, leaders cannot delegate the solving of problems to someone else. They have to be active in breaking through obstacles, putting out fires, correcting mistakes, and directing people. Leaders on the Production level do that. And once their effectiveness becomes contagious and spreads throughout the team, productivity begins to solve many problems — many more than management or consultants ever will.

Historian and essayist Thomas Carlyle observed, "Nothing builds self-esteem and self-confidence like accomplishment." Productivity is inspiring. People who feel good about themselves often produce good results. And good results create positive momentum and high morale.

> "Nothing builds self-esteem and self-confidence like accomplishment."
> —*Thomas Carlyle*

For years I wondered which comes first: high morale or high productivity. I have heard good arguments for both sides of this chicken-or-egg question. I have seen high morale stimulate production. I have also seen productivity create high morale. I can't say that it always happens one way, but here is what I do know: remove production and high morale will fade fast. Keep producing, and high morale will continue for a long time.

Leaders who can produce positive results on Level 3 always have a positive impact on their team. Leaders who can't produce always hurt their team. In the War of 1812, the American general William Winder led his forces to defeat against the British—despite a four-to-one troop superiority. In the process, he was taken prisoner. However, realizing that Winder's incompetence made him an ideal opponent, the British returned him to the American army. As a result, when the British later attacked the American capital, they were able to overcome defending forces led by Winder and burn much of it to the ground. If Winder had been able to advance to Level 3 in leadership prior to taking command as a general, perhaps his men could have stopped the British army's advances in battle. As it was, he succeeded only in hurting the American cause.

Productive organizations led by Level 3 leaders are hard to beat. Their effectiveness is high, and so is their morale. Former general George C. Marshall said, "Morale is the state of mind. It is steadfastness and courage and hope. It is confidence and zeal and loyalty.... It is staying power, the spirit which endures to the end—the will to win. With it all things are possible, without it everything else...is for naught."

5. Leadership Production Creates Momentum

When well-led organizations sustain high morale and high productivity over time, they gain momentum, which is any leader's best friend. Momentum helps a leader do anything and everything more easily. That's why I call it the great exaggerator. Without momentum, everything is harder to do than it should be. With it, everything is easier.

My wife and I live in coastal Florida on a river that flows into the ocean about a mile from our house. So every day we witness the ebb and flow of the tide. I sometimes enjoy swimming in the river, and I've made a discovery. When I'm swimming with the tide, my progress has little to do with the speed and strength of my strokes. It is determined by how fast the tide is moving. Swim with it and you make fast progress. Swim against it and you move very slowly, no matter how hard you work at it. When the tide is up, all the boats rise. When it is down, all the boats go down. It's hard to fight the tide.

The same can be said of leadership momentum. Have it on your side, and your performance is actually better than your capability. For example, think about what happened with Apple when the company introduced the iPhone. It created a tidal wave of momentum and vastly increased their market share, not only in smartphones but also in computers. After years of being marginalized as a niche company with a relatively small but very loyal following, they are now mainstream again and going strong. That's why I often advise leaders to spend less time trying to fix problems and more trying to create momentum.

Level 3 is a momentum-producing environment. Production-level leaders understand momentum and use it to the organization's advantage. And they also understand that not everyone in an organization helps to create momentum. Here's what I mean. There are three types of people when it comes to momentum. They are:

Momentum Takers

The vast majority of people don't start anything, nor do they stop anything. They just go along for the ride. If momentum is moving, they move with it. If it has stopped, so do they. Their productivity and effectiveness are based almost entirely on what others do to make things happen in the organization. For that reason, they need good leaders who produce and create a productive environment. That is one of the reasons that I define morale as "faith in the leader."

> I define morale as "faith in the leader."

Momentum Breakers

The second type of person actually hurts morale and momentum in an organization. Not only do they not produce, but they prevent others from producing. These types of people cause problems and, whether intentionally or not, hurt the organization.

Momentum Makers

The final type, momentum makers, are Level 3 leaders. They produce. They make things happen. They create momentum. Their behavior is consistent with the advice given by the legendary Alabama football coach Paul "Bear" Bryant, who said, "Don't worry about making friends; don't worry about making enemies. Worry about winning, because if you win, your enemies can't hurt you, and if you lose, your friends can't stand you."

> "Don't worry about making friends; don't worry about making enemies. Worry about winning, because if you win, your enemies can't hurt you, and if you lose, your friends can't stand you."
> —Paul "Bear" Bryant

If you build solid permissional relationships on top of a foundation of positional rights and add the results of productivity, you will gain momentum. And when you do, you'll find that your work comes to fruition more quickly. That is a benefit of Level 3.

6. Leadership Production is the Foundation for Team-Building

Who wants to leave a championship team? No one! Who wants to leave the cellar dweller? Everyone! People simply love being on a winning team.

Winners attract people—some good, some bad, some average. The key to building a winning team is recognizing, selecting, and retaining the best people from the ones you attract. The good news is that if you reach Level 3, you know what productivity looks like because you live it. The bad news is that having talented people on the team doesn't automatically guarantee success. You can still lose with good players, but you cannot win without them. The difference comes from building them into a team, which I'll discuss later in the chapter. But remember this: if you aren't a proven producer, you won't attract and keep other proven producers. That's why you need to win Level 3.

The Downside of Production

The Weight of Leadership Just Got Heavier

Like everything else in life, the Production level of leadership has its downsides as well as its upsides. With Level 3 leadership, achievement within the organization becomes easier. However, the leadership itself doesn't become easy. Here are the four main downsides I've discovered on Level 3:

1. Being Productive Can Make You Think You're a Leader When You're Not

All great leaders are productive. However, it is possible to be a producer and not a leader. Personal success does not always translate into team success. Leadership is defined by what a person does with and for others. It is established by making the team better and more productive. It's measured by what the entire group accomplishes, not by the individual efforts of the person in charge. Good leadership is never based on what someone does by and for himself.

I know many individual producers who have no desire or ability to lead others. Some don't have the people skills. Others don't have the desire to be responsible for others or take the time to help them become productive. For example, Ted Williams was one of the greatest hitters in baseball. He is the last player to have a batting average over .400

during a season. Yet he was not a successful hitting coach. When his players were not hitting well, he would say, "Keep your eye on the ball." That advice was given by a man with extraordinary coordination, who was successful because he was able to look at a ball and tell what kind of pitch it was by how the stitching moved. In his mind, it was all simple. All he did was keep his eye on the ball. His players, who were less talented, needed more instruction. Ted Williams was a great player, but he never made it as a leader in baseball.

Organizations all over the world make the mistake of putting high producers into leadership positions only to watch them fail to lead well. I've done that. I've seen someone make things happen, and I thought, *Wow, this person is going to be a fantastic leader,* only to have that person continue to make things happen for himself but ignore and demoralize his team. That's not leadership.

Why is this mistake made so often? Because a prerequisite for being an effective leader is the ability to be effective yourself. That is one of the qualifying marks of a leader, but it is not the only qualification. Good leaders must establish themselves in their position on Level 1, gain people's permission on Level 2, be productive on Level 3, *and* possess the desire to take the entire team to a higher level.

2. Productive Leaders Feel a Heavy Weight of Responsibility for Results

I once saw a cartoon depicting a sales meeting in which the speaker said, "We run our business like a game show — produce and you come back, don't produce and we have some lovely parting gifts for you." That's humorous, but that's also the way it is for leaders. If a football team doesn't win, the coach gets fired. If a corporation doesn't make profits, the CEO gets the ax. If a politician doesn't do a good job for his constituents, he doesn't get reelected. In any organization, the responsibility for results rests with the leaders. What the World War II British field marshal Bernard Law Montgomery said was true: "No leader, however great, can long continue unless he wins victories."

> "No leader, however great, can long continue unless he wins victories."
> —*Bernard Law Montgomery*

Productivity is measurable. Organizational growth is tangible. Profitability is quantifiable. Leaders who fail to increase them are held accountable. Leaders who add to them are rewarded—and then asked to achieve even more the next time. High performance requires high commitment.

Honestly, many leaders who reach Level 3 tire of leading because of the weight of responsibility they feel. Most leaders experience days when they wish no one was watching their performance, looking to them for direction, or wanting them to make something happen. However, effective leaders understand that the cost of leadership is carrying the responsibility of their team's success on their shoulders. That is a weight every leader feels starting on Level 3. You will have to decide whether you are willing to carry it.

3. Production Leadership Requires Making Difficult Decisions

A large corporation recently made a stray dog a senior vice-president. When asked why they would do such a thing, the board of directors replied, "His ability to get along with anyone, his prompt response to a pat on the back, his interest in watching others work, and his great knack for looking wise while saying nothing made him a natural for the position." If only leadership were that easy!

Whenever you see a thriving organization, you can be sure that its leaders made some very tough decisions—and are continuing to make them. Success is an uphill journey. People don't coast their way to effective leadership. As billionaire oilman and environmental advocate T. Boone Pickens says, "Be willing to make decisions. That's the most important quality in a good leader."

If you want to lead at a higher level, be ready to make difficult decisions. On Level 2, leaders often have to start making difficult people decisions. On Level 3, leaders continue to make those but also add difficult production decisions. That makes leadership even more difficult. I've already told you about how difficult I found it to make decisions early in my career. You may find it helpful to know that today as I look back, I regret the decisions I failed to make more than I do the wrong decisions I did make. Don't fall into the same trap I did of postponing decisions when I should have made them.

> Today as I look back, I regret the decisions I failed to make more than I do the wrong decisions I did make.

What kinds of difficult decisions are leaders likely to make on Level 3? Most of them will be decisions you must make related to yourself! I found that about 25 percent of the decisions I make on Level 3 relate to my team. The rest are personal ones that require change, honesty, and self-discipline. As the American writer Mark Twain said, "To do right is wonderful. To teach others to do right is even more wonderful—and much easier." That is so true.

As a leader on Level 3, you must make the Difficult Decision to...

- Be successful *before* you try to help others be successful.
- Hold yourself to a higher standard than you ask of others.
- Make yourself accountable to others.
- Set tangible goals and then reach them.
- Accept responsibility for personal results.
- Admit failure and mistakes quickly and humbly.
- Ask from others only what you have previously asked of yourself.
- Gauge your success on results, not intentions.
- Remove yourself from situations where you are ineffective.

It has been my observation that when leaders are confronted with these difficult decisions on Level 3, many fail to make them. What they may not understand until it's too late is that failing to do so will eventually disqualify them from leading themselves or others. Their leadership potential becomes stunted, and they cannot remain on Level 3.

> "To do right is wonderful. To teach others to do right is even more wonderful—and much easier."
> —*Mark Twain*

I can remember facing each of these decisions on Level 3. It took me a long time to make some of them. It certainly wasn't easy. Sometimes it still isn't. But each decision created a personal breakthrough in my leadership journey.

I encourage you to win in this area of your leadership life. Persevere—even in moments when you feel the way Moses must have when the Red Sea parted and the people waited for him to take them forward, saying to himself, *Why must I always go first?* Going first may not always be easy or fun, but it is always a requirement of leaders. It paves the way for the people who follow and increases their chances of success for completing the journey.

4. Production Leadership Demands Continual Attention to Level 2

Becoming accountable for the productivity of the team does not mean that leaders can stop caring for the people they lead. Remember, just because you add a new level of leadership doesn't mean you leave the previous one behind.

There is a real temptation for leaders on the Production level to neglect relationships in pursuit of achieving a good bottom-line result. However, if leaders do that for an extended period of time, they burn their relationships with their people, and they will eventually find themselves back on Level 1. Don't fall into that trap. Keep developing the relationships and caring for them as you produce results.

Best Behaviors on Level 3

How to Make the Most of Production in Leadership

Moving up through Level 3 based upon solid Level 2 relationships is no small feat for any person. Many people find themselves incapable of achieving it. If you have the opportunity, here is what you need to do to make the most of it:

1. Understand How Your Personal Giftedness Contributes to the Vision

One of the keys to the Production level of leadership is understanding how your gifts and abilities can be used productively to further the vision of the organization. Part of that is personal. In previous chapters I discussed the importance of knowing yourself and deciding on your personal leadership style. This is slightly different. If you are a leader, you must have a sense of vision for your leadership. And it must align, at least during the current season, with the vision of the organization you serve.

It took me a long time to develop a sense of where my true strengths lie and how I can serve an organization that I lead. Discovering it took effort, and the process was often messy. But eventually I came to understand that I had special gifts and abilities. (So do you.) There is a strong relationship between giftedness and effectiveness as a leader on the Production level. If I ever wanted to reach my potential as a leader, I had to know what my personal contribution could be to the organization. The same is true for you.

As an example, I'll tell you the four areas where I personally contribute the most to the productivity of an organization or a team:

- Influencing People (Leadership)
- Connecting with People (Relationships)
- Communicating with People (Speaking)
- Creating Resources to Help People (Writing)

These comprise my strength zone. These are the key to production for me and where the best results will be realized.

Knowing this doesn't let me off the hook as far as growth and learning are concerned. I am as committed to learning and growing today as I was back in the early 1970s, when I started my first personal growth plan. The difference is that I now concentrate almost exclusively on growing in those four areas. After discovering what I was made to do, I began to focus my efforts.

The more focused you are within your talents, the more rapid the rate of growth and the greater you increase your overall potential to be a productive leader. If you want to maximize your ability on Level 3, you need to follow the advice of Walt Disney, who said, "Do what you do so well that those who see you do what you do are going to come back to see you do it again and tell others that they should see you do what you do."

If you want your team or department to be good at what they do, then you need to become good at what you do. Productivity has to start with the leader. Focus there first, and you will earn opportunities to help others improve and reach their potential.

2. Cast Vision for What Needs to Be Accomplished

Vision casting is an integral part of leading. Fuzzy communication leads to unclear direction, which produces sloppy execution. Productive leaders create a clear link between the vision of the organization and everyday production of the team. They show how the short term impacts the long term. They are clear in their communication and continually point the way for their team.

A compelling vision is clear and well-defined, expansive and challenging. It is aligned with the shared values of the team. It is focused primarily on the end, not means. It fits the giftedness of the team. And when it is communicated and understood, it fills the room with energy!

How do leaders give their teams the greatest possible success in achieving the vision? By helping team members to do three things:

Level 3 Leaders Help People Define the Success of the Vision

In every organization I have led, I found it necessary to define or redefine what success meant for the people working there. For example, when I owned Injoy Stewardship Services, it meant working to help churches raise money to advance their vision. When I founded EQUIP, it meant working to bring long-term leadership development to every country in the world and give local leaders resources in their own languages. When I created the John Maxwell Company, it meant developing resources and teaching coaching skills to people who wanted to add value to others. How in the world can an organization be successful if the people in it don't know what the target is?

Level 3 Leaders Help People Commit to the Success of the Vision

The commitment of the team begins with the commitment of the leader. Teams don't win unless their leaders are determined to do everything they can to succeed, to dedicate their productivity to advancing the organization toward the vision. Once they have committed to use

> The commitment of the team begins with the commitment of the leader.

their time, talents, and resources to achieve the vision, they gain credibility and their people gain the confidence to follow suit. Only then has the groundwork been laid for team building.

Level 3 Leaders Help People Experience Success

Few things inspire people like victory. The job of a leader is to help the team succeed. As individuals on the team get to experience small successes, it motivates them to keep going and reach for larger successes. If you want your people to be inspired to win, then reward and celebrate the small daily victories that they achieve. And make them part of your personal victory celebrations whenever possible, giving them as much of the credit as you can. Not only does that motivate people, but it also helps them to enjoy the journey.

3. Begin to Develop Your People into a Team

When you get to Level 2 with people in your organization, they begin to like *being* together. But when you get to Level 3, they begin to *work* together. Production makes team building possible. That can be accomplished only by a leader who is willing to push forward and lead the way for the people.

In his book *Principle-Centered Leadership*, Stephen M. R. Covey tells how Columbus was once invited to a banquet, where he was assigned the most honorable place at the table. A shallow courtier who was meanly jealous of him asked abruptly: "Had you not discovered the Indies, are there not other men in Spain who would have been capable of the enterprise?"

Columbus made no reply but took an egg and invited the company to make it stand on end. They all attempted, but in vain; whereupon he tapped it on the table, denting one end, and left it standing.

"We all could have done it that way!" the courtier accused.

"Yes, if you had only known how," retorted Columbus. "And once I showed you the way to the New World, nothing was easier than to follow it."

Team building is one of my favorite aspects of leading people. Why? Because a good team is always greater than the sum of its parts and is able to accomplish more than individuals working alone. Working as a team is also just plain fun! I love teamwork and team building so much that I've written a few books on it, including *The 17 Indisputable Laws of Teamwork*. There's a lot to say about teamwork—more than I have space for here. But I want to give you some critical things to think about related to team building as you strive to become good at leading on Level 3 (and I've listed the Laws of Teamwork that apply to each for your reference):

Team Members Should Complement One Another— Team Leaders Should Make That Happen

Author Stephen Covey asserted, "The job of a leader is to build a complementary team, where every strength is made effective and each weakness is made irrelevant." That is the ideal that every leader should shoot for— people working together, each bringing their strengths to make the team better and compensating for each other's weaknesses. How does that happen? First, you must know the strengths and weaknesses of each player.

> "The job of a leader is to build a complementary team, where every strength is made effective and each weakness is made irrelevant."
> —*Stephen Covey*

John Wooden, the great UCLA basketball coach, once told me, "Most of my college players shot for a higher percentage at UCLA than they did in high school." I played basketball, so I knew it was unusual for a player to move in that direction when going to a higher level.

"How did you accomplish that?" I asked.

"The first few days of basketball practice," he explained, "I would observe the players shooting the ball from various places on the court. When I determined the place they made the best percentage of shots, 'their spot,' I would take them to that place and say, 'This is where I want you to shoot the ball. I will design plays to make sure that happens.'"

Coach Wooden would also point out places on the floor where they needed to pass the ball instead of shoot it. In this way, he made the most of a strength (by having them shoot) and turned a potential weakness into a strength (by having them pass to someone in their place of strength). That practice really sheds light on one of Wooden's most famous quotes: "The one who scores a basket has ten hands." In other words, it takes all the players to help one player make a basket. And it takes a leader to help them figure out how to do it and lead them through the process.

> "The one who scores a basket has ten hands."
> —John Wooden

Applicable Laws of Teamwork

The Law of Significance: One Is Too Small a Number to Achieve Greatness

The Law of Mount Everest: As the Challenge Escalates, the Need for Teamwork Elevates

The Law of the Catalyst: Winning Teams Have Players Who Make Things Happen

The Law of the Bench: Great Teams Have Great Depth

The Law of Dividends: Investing in the Team Compounds over Time

Team Members Should Understand Their Mission— Team Leaders Should Make That Happen

Good leaders never assume that their team members understand the mission. They don't take anything for granted. No doubt that was the reason the legendary NFL coach Vince Lombardi's first speech every season began with the sentence, "This is a football." It's the reason Coach Wooden taught his players at the beginning of every season the proper way to put on socks so that they wouldn't sustain foot injuries. They made sure their players knew what they needed to in order to accomplish their mission.

As you lead people on Level 3, don't take for granted that they know what you know or believe what you believe. Don't assume they understand how their talents and efforts are supposed to contribute to the mission of the team. Communicate it often.

Applicable Laws of Teamwork

The Law of the Big Picture: The Goal Is More Important Than the Role

The Law of the Niche: All Players Have a Place Where They Add the Most Value

The Law of the Compass: Vision Gives Team Members Direction and Confidence

The Law of the Price Tag: The Team Fails to Reach Its Potential When It Fails to Pay the Price

Team Members Should Receive Feedback about Their Performance—Team Leaders Should Make That Happen

I sometimes speak about a basketball coach who had a regular practice during halftime to help the team prepare for the second half. On a whiteboard in the locker room, the coach would write three columns: Did Right—Did Wrong—Will Change. A friend of mine who runs a business heard the story and decided to do that with her company at the midpoint of the year, calling it the organization's halftime.

She went into the meeting prepared, having made a list of her own for each of the columns. But being an effective leader on Level 3, the first thing she did was ask all the people on her team to share their observations. She added her own items to their list only when no one else mentioned them, which was rare. The meeting was a success. Here's what she discovered as a result:

- She was not leading by assumption. She knew where her team stood and what they thought about the work they did during the first six months.
- She gained a new perspective and learned things she didn't know. This allowed her and the team to be on the same page.
- The team was able to make halftime adjustments before it was too late. The same kind of meeting at the end of the year would not have had the same benefits.
- The team took ownership of the rest of the year because their ideas had come from the heart. They were the ones who came up with what was on the whiteboard.

The process was so effective that it became a regular event every year. People always want to know how they're doing. They want to succeed. And if they're not succeeding, most of the time they want to know how to make adjustments to improve. Most people are willing to change if they are convinced that changing will help them win. Productive leaders take responsibility for walking team members through that process.

Applicable Laws of Teamwork

The Law of the Chain: The Strength of the Team Is Impacted by Its Weakest Link

The Law of the Bad Apple: Rotten Attitudes Ruin a Team

The Law of Countability: Teammates Must Be Able to Count on Each Other When It Counts

The Law of the Scoreboard: The Team Can Make Adjustments When It Knows Where It Stands

Team Members Should Work in an Environment Conducive to Growth and Inspiration—Team Leaders Should Make That Happen

A few years ago while Margaret and I were in Venice, we visited a former palace in which there was a large room where 1,500 leaders met periodically to make important decisions. Our guide pointed out the beautiful paintings on every wall. Each painting represented a specific time in the city's history in which the Venetian leaders had achieved a significant victory because of a courageous decision and subsequent action. We were both inspired. It reminded me how important it is for leaders to create an environment for their people that inspires, challenges, and stretches them.

As you lead on Level 3, you need to make it your goal to lift up others and help them do their best. Founding Father Benjamin Franklin was a leader who understood this. In a letter written to John Paul Jones, Franklin gave the new officer advice concerning how to lead others:

> Hereafter, if you should observe an occasion to give your officers and friends a little more praise than is their due, and confess more fault than you justly be charged with, you will only become the sooner for it, a great captain. Criticizing and censuring almost everyone you have to do with, will diminish friends, increase enemies, and thereby hurt your affairs.

Franklin's wisdom is as valid today as it was then. He knew how to create a work environment conducive to growth and inspiration. Effective leaders on Level 3 do this well. It is a key to productivity.

I have sometimes been criticized as a leader for being too positive and praising people more than I should. I think that criticism is justified. There have been times when I have built up people on my team more than their performance has warranted, and it has come back to bite me. Believing the best in people usually has a positive return, but sometimes it doesn't. High faith in people is both a strength and a weakness of mine. But it's a weakness I'm willing to live with because the usual benefits are so high. Besides, I'd rather live as a positive person and occasionally get burned than be constantly skeptical and negative. I believe that to a large extent you get what you expect in life. I don't want to expect the worst for myself or anyone else. People need a positive environment to be productive and thrive.

The leaders set the tone more than anyone else on a team, in a department, or for an organization. Their attitude is contagious. If they are positive, encouraging, and open to growth, so are their people. If you want to succeed on Level 3, acknowledge the influence you have and use it to everyone's best advantage.

Applicable Laws of Teamwork

The Law of Identity: Shared Values Define the Team

The Law of Communication: Interaction Fuels Action

The Law of the Edge: The Difference Between Two Equally Talented Teams Is Leadership

The Law of High Morale: When You're Winning, Nothing Hurts

Developing a group of people into a productive team is no easy task. If it were, every professional sports team would be a winner and every business would earn high profits. It's a challenge to get everybody working together to achieve a common vision. But it is definitely worth the effort. Being part of a team of people doing something of high value is one of the most rewarding experiences in life. As a leader, you have a chance to help people experience it. Don't shrink from that great opportunity.

4. Prioritize the Things That Yield High Return

What's the key to being productive? Prioritizing. To be an effective Level 3 leader, you must learn to not only get a lot done, but to get a lot of the right things done. That means understanding how to prioritize time, tasks, resources, and even people.

Jim Collins, author of *Good to Great*, asserts that effective prioritizing begins with eliminating the things you shouldn't be doing. He writes,

> Most of us lead busy but undisciplined lives. We have ever-expanding "to do" lists, trying to build momentum by doing, doing, doing—and doing more. And it rarely works. Those who build the good-to-great companies, however, made as much use of "stop doing" lists as "to do" lists. They displayed a remarkable discipline to unplug all sorts of extraneous junk.[4]

Truly, the best companies channel their resources into only a few arenas—ones where they can be successful.

Staying in your areas of strength—where your efforts yield the highest return—and out of your areas of weakness is one of the keys to personal productivity. And if you can help others on

> Effective prioritizing begins with eliminating the things you shouldn't be doing.

your team to do the same, then you can be successful in leadership on Level 3. For years I have relied on the Pareto Principle as a guideline to help me decide what is worth focusing on and what isn't. The Pareto Principle basically says that if you do the top 20 percent of your to-do list, it will yield you an 80 percent return on your efforts.

To help me understand what my top 20 percent is, I ask myself three questions:

- What is required of me? (what I must do)
- What gives me the greatest return? (what I should do)
- What is most rewarding to me? (what I love to do)

If you are early in your career or new to leadership, your must-do list will probably be the largest. Your goal as you climb the levels of leadership, is to shift your time and attention to the should-dos and love-to-dos. And if you lead well enough for long enough and build a great team, the answers for all three questions should be the same things. I feel very fortunate because that has come to pass for me. There are relatively few things I am required to do that I don't enjoy doing.

As you lead your team, your goal should be to help every person get to the place where they are doing their should-dos and love-to-dos, because that is where they will be most effective. As a rule of thumb, try to hire, train, and position people in such a way that

80 percent of the time they work in their strength zone;
15 percent of the time they work in a learning zone;
 5 percent of the time they work outside their strength zone; and
 0 percent of the time they work in their weakness zone.

To facilitate that, you must really know your people, understand their strengths and weaknesses, and be willing to have candid conversations with them. If you've done your work on Level 2, then you should be ready, willing, and able to do those things.

5. Be Willing and Ready to Be a Change Agent

Progress always requires change. That's a fact. Most leaders desire to create progress. It's one of the things that make them tick. However, only when leaders reach Level 3 are they in a place where they can start to effect change. Why is that? Well, your position is established as a leader on Level 1. You've built strong relationships with people on your team on Level 2. And once you've helped the team to achieve some results on Level 3, you've got the credibility and the momentum to start making changes. It's very diffi-cult to make changes when an organiza-tion is standing still. Get it going in *any* direction and you will find it easier to make changes to move it in the *right* direction. Momentum provides the energy for needed change.

> Momentum provides the energy for needed change.

Change in an organization is always a leadership issue. It takes a leader to create positive change. And the best way to start working as a change agent is the same as when trying to build a relationship. You need to find common ground. Any leader who wants to make changes is tempted to point out differences and try to convince others why change is needed. But that rarely works. Instead, focus on the similari-ties and build upon those. To get started, look for common ground in the following areas:

- **Vision:** When the vision is similar, you can bet that the people are standing together and they have the same view. If their vision is similar to yours, you all see it clearly, and everyone has a strong desire to see it come to fruition, you can probably work well together.
- **Values:** It's difficult to travel with others very long if your val-ues don't align. Find out what others stand for and try to meet where you share the same standards.
- **Relationships:** Great teams have people who are as committed to one another as they are to the vision. If you've done the work on Level 2, you should already share common ground in this area.

- **Attitude:** If you are going to get people to work together for positive change, their attitudes need to be positive and tenacious. If they're not, there will be trouble ahead.
- **Communication:** For change to occur, communication must be open, honest, and ongoing. When people are in the dark, they start to speculate about what's happening. And their assumptions are often wrong. Inform people so that everyone is on the same page.

If you can find or create common ground in these five areas, you can move forward and introduce change. That doesn't necessarily mean that being a change agent will be easy. But I can guarantee that if you don't win those five areas, change will be very difficult.

6. Never Lose Sight of the Fact That Results Are Your Goal

There's a big difference between Level 3 leaders and critics who simply theorize about productivity. Good leaders have an orientation toward results. They know that results always matter—regardless of how many obstacles they face, what the economy does, what kinds of problems their people experience, and so on. They fight for productivity and are held accountable no matter what. Even when they experience success! Automaker Henry Ford observed,

> More men are failures on account of success than on account of failures. They beat their way over a dozen obstacles, overcome a host of difficulties, sacrifice and sweat. They make the impossible the possible; then along comes a little success, and it tumbles them from their perch. They let up, they slip and over they go. Nobody can count the number of people who have been halted and beaten by recognition and reward![5]

Good leaders on Level 3 keep pushing. If they gain momentum, they don't back off and coast. They press on and increase the momentum so that they can accomplish even greater things. And they help their people do the same. How are they able to stay focused and accomplish so much—despite success as well as failure? Once again Henry Ford has a suggestion. "Make your future plans so long and so hard," Ford advised, "that the people who praise you will always seem to you to be talking about something very trivial in comparison with what you are really trying to do. It is better to have a job too big for popular praise, so big that you can get a good start on it before the cheer squad can get its first intelligent glimmering of your plans. Then you will be free to work and continue your journey towards even greater success."

Leaders who reach Level 3 always experience success. But not all of them capitalize on that success and go to the next level. To do that, they have to remain focused and productive—all while cultivating and preserving positive relationships. And the really good ones use the Production level as a platform for Level 4, where they develop other people to become good leaders in their own right.

The Laws of Leadership at the Production Level

If you want to use the Laws of Leadership to help you grow and win Permission on Level 3, then consider the following:

The Law of Respect
People Naturally Follow Leaders Stronger Than Themselves

People do not naturally follow people whose leadership is weaker than their own. People follow others they respect, people who have credibility. If they recognize that someone else's success is greater than their own, then they gladly follow that person's lead. Why? Because what that leader has done for the organization is very likely to spill over into the life and work of the person following. It's a win for everyone involved.

When you're working to gain relational credibility on Level 2, the positive results are often intangibles, such as morale and trust. In contrast, the results of good leadership are highly tangible at Level 3. People see better organization, increased productivity, and higher profitability. The result is that they see your strengths and understand what you can do. Your credibility is established. People respect that, and they follow not only because you treat people well, but because of what you do for the team and organization.

The Law of Magnetism
Who You Are Is Who You Attract

In general, people attract others similar to themselves. Birds of a feather flock together. Often I ask leaders to list the three or four characteristics they most desire in their team members. After they have decided on them, I ask a question: "Do you possess those same characteristics?" Why? Because if we don't exhibit them, we won't attract them. We tend not to attract who we want. We attract who we are.

When you reach Level 3 and create a highly productive team, you begin to attract other producers. The great thing about this is that it helps you to make the productive team you've developed even more productive. Introducing additional highly productive people to the team raises the bar and makes everyone more productive. And if there are people on the team who won't or can't produce, others will be lined up at your door willing to take their place.

The Law of the Picture
People Do What People See

Leaders are usually highly visible to the people they lead, especially if they lead by going first. As a result, their actions are always noticed. If you're a producer, that's a good thing. Nothing motivates people in a positive way more than seeing a positive leadership model. When people see results from their leaders, they know results are expected from them. And whenever results are an expectation, greater productivity happens. Good leaders on Level 3 know that they are showing the way by going the way because people do what people see.

> Nothing motivates people in a positive way more than seeing a positive leadership model.

The Law of Victory
Leaders Find a Way for the Team to Win

If you were going to play basketball and you could choose anyone in the world to be on the same team with you, who would you pick? How about if you were playing football? Or if you were going into business? Or starting a nonprofit? Chances are the people you listed are the top leaders in their fields. Why would you want them on your team? Because your odds of winning go through the roof when you're teamed with a leader who has a track record for finding ways to win.

The best leaders on Level 3 find ways to win. They always do. They produce! And they do so day in and day out, regardless of the odds, obstacles, or circumstances. If you are one of those people who consistently produces, then everyone will want to be on your team. That makes leading that much better.

The Law of the Big Mo
Momentum Is a Leader's Best Friend

Leadership is easier at Level 3 than Level 2. Why? Level 3 is where momentum kicks in. Good results create momentum. Having momentum gives you greater results. Greater results create even more momentum. Production creates a positive cycle that can continue to roll on and on. With momentum, an organization can overcome problems, negativism, past issues, pettiness, and upcoming obstacles.

If you find yourself on Level 3 gaining momentum, it's not time to have a rest or back off. It's time to press on. Never take momentum for granted. Keep giving your all. As Jim Collins might say, keep the flywheel moving.

The Law of Priorities
Leaders Understand That Activity Is Not Necessarily Accomplishment

According to a well-known seller of daily planners, only a third of American workers plan their daily schedules, and fewer than 10 percent of people complete what they do plan. That's not very encouraging.

Most leaders feel a great deal of pressure to get a lot of work done. Productive leaders understand that activity is not necessarily accomplishment. It's very easy for people to work hard all day every day, and never get done the important things that make themselves and their teams productive. What's the key? Prioritizing. Level 3 leaders do the right things the right way at the right time for the right reasons. They know that an organization where anything goes eventually becomes a company where nothing goes. They plan and act accordingly.

The Law of Sacrifice
A Leader Must Give Up to Go Up

Radio broadcaster Paul Harvey remarked, "You can tell you're on the road to success; it's uphill all the way." Climbing to the higher levels of leadership isn't easy. It takes effort. It also requires sacrifices. You won't be able to win one level using the skills you used to win the last one. You'll have to give up some privileges and resources to move up. You'll have to give up doing some of the things you love that don't give a great enough return on your time. And some people you'd love to take with you to the top will refuse to go.

> "You can tell you're on the road to success; it's uphill all the way."
> —*Paul Harvey*

Leaders learn to let go of everything but the essentials as they climb. No leader who made it to the top ever said, "It was easier than I thought and took less time." As you work to climb higher, prepare yourself for the sacrifices you'll have to make to become a better leader.

The Law of Buy-In
People Buy into the Leader, Then the Vision

Most leaders have a vision for where they're going and how their team can accomplish something they believe in. Do you have a vision? How do you know whether your team members will buy into it? By knowing whether they already buy into you!

People buy into the leader, then the vision. That buy-in comes from two things: the relationship you have with them and the results you demonstrated in front of them. They want to know you care about them, and they want to know you can produce. They learn both of those things from watching you and seeing your example. When they enjoy you as a person and perceive you as a producer, then they have what they need to buy in.

Beliefs That Help a Leader Move Up to Level 4

Leadership is an exciting journey. The most talented and dedicated leaders feel the pull to go higher. They hear a call to continually grow and help others do the same. Their beliefs give them the incentive to climb, but their behaviors are what actually take them to the next level.

If you want to go to that next level, then embrace the following ideas while still on Level 3:

1. Production Is Not Enough

Leading a productive team is quite an accomplishment. Achieving goals can be very rewarding. But there are higher levels of leadership than just getting work done effectively and adding to the bottom line. What's better than excellence at your work and high productivity from your team? Developing people so that they can lead with you. Great leaders measure themselves by what they get done through others. That requires developing people in a leadership culture. That is the focus of leaders on Level 4.

> Great leaders measure themselves by what they get done through others. That requires developing people in a leadership culture.

For many years I was satisfied to be a Level 3 leader. To be honest, when I first learned to be a productive leader on Level 3, I thought I had arrived at the highest level of leadership. I enjoyed producing and developing my team. But then I felt the pull to go higher. I realized that I could do more. I could develop people to become excellent leaders in their own right. If I did, not only would I increase the capacity of the organization and lighten my personal leadership load, but I would also add value to people in a way that would really benefit them. That soon became my focus — and my greatest joy.

If you have reached Level 3 with your team members and you lead a productive team, congratulations. You've achieved more than most people ever do. But don't settle for Production. Seek the higher levels where you can help change people's lives.

2. People Are an Organization's Most Appreciable Asset

Most of what an organization possesses goes down in value. Facilities deteriorate. Equipment becomes out of date. Supplies get used up. What asset has the greatest potential for actually going up in value? People! But only if they are valued, challenged, and developed by someone capable of investing in them and helping them grow. Otherwise, they are like money put on deposit without interest. Their potential is high, but they aren't actually growing.

People don't appreciate automatically or grow accidentally. Growth occurs only when it's intentional. Where does growth happen on the 5 Levels of Leadership? On Level 4. It is on this level that leaders engage in People Development. If you want to go to the next level in your leadership, think beyond Production and start thinking in terms of how you can help the individuals on your team to improve themselves and tap into their potential.

3. Growing Leaders Is the Most Effective Way to
Accomplish the Vision

How do you make an organization better? Invest in the people who work in it. Companies get better when their people get better. That's why investing in people always gives a greater return to an organization.

> Companies get better when their people get better. That's why investing in people always gives a greater return to an organization.

Everything rises and falls on leadership. The more leaders an organization has, the greater its horsepower. The better leaders an organization has, the greater its potential. You cannot overinvest in people. Every time you increase the ability of a person in the organization, you increase the ability to fulfill the vision. Everything gets better when good leaders are leading the organization and creating a positive, productive work environment.

If you want a pleasant work environment, win Level 2. If you want a productive work environment, win Level 3. If you want a *growing* work environment, win Level 4.

4. People Development Is the Greatest
Fulfillment for a Leader

When I was in my late thirties, I found myself trying to accomplish a large vision that required more of me than I was capable of giving on my own. The only solution I could see was to train and develop other people to help carry the load. But then something wonderful happened. What started as a necessity soon became the greatest source of fulfillment in my life.

Few things in life are better than seeing people reach their potential. If you help people become bigger and better on the inside, eventually they will become greater on the outside. People are like trees: give them what they need to grow on a continual basis for long enough, and they will grow from the inside out. And they will bear fruit.

> It is impossible to help others without helping yourself.

If you invest in people, they will never be the same again. And neither will you. It is impossible to help others without helping yourself.

Guide to Growing through Level 3

As you reflect on the upsides, downsides, best behaviors, and beliefs related to the Production level of leadership, use the following guidelines to help you grow as a leader:

1. **Be the Team Member You Want on Your Team:** Some leaders make the same mistake as some parents. They expect people to do as they say, not as they do. But here's the problem: people do what people see. If you want dedicated, thoughtful, productive people on your team, you must model those characteristics. Take time to list all the qualities you desire in your team members. Then compare your own personal qualities to those on the list. Wherever you don't measure up, next to the characteristic write an action statement describing what you must do to possess the trait you'd like to see. For example, if you want people to be dedicated, then write, "I will not give up solving a problem or doing a task until it is completed," or "I will arrive early and stay late to set an example for the team."

   > Some leaders make the same mistake as some parents. They expect people to do as they say, not as they do.

2. **Translate Personal Productivity into Leadership:** Just because you have a history of being a productive individual doesn't necessarily mean you are a Production level leader.

How can you tell the difference? The evidence can be found in your impact on the rest of the team. Are other members of the team improving or producing more as a result of your presence? If not, why not? Think about the things you could do to help others become better, both individually and as a team. Turn your focus outward from your own production and begin helping others to become high producers.

3. **Understand Everyone's Productivity Niche:** One of the hallmarks of successful Level 3 leaders is knowing not only where they add the greatest value to the team, but where everyone else adds value, too. Take some time to define each team member's area of contribution (including your own), and figure out how they all work together to make the team most effective.

4. **Cast Vision Continually:** When was the last time you cast vision to your team? Unless it was today, you're probably overdue. Team members need you to describe the vision and define its success. Take time to carefully craft your communication, and deliver it creatively as often as possible.

5. **Build Your Team:** As team members come to understand the vision and begin to learn their strengths and roles, they can be formed into a productive team. That can be accomplished by creating a growth and performance environment. Plan to meet with your team daily (or at least weekly) to give feedback on performance. Do not penalize risk taking. Praise people's effort, help them learn from their failures, and reward their successes.

6. **Use Momentum to Solve Problems:** What's the most effective way to solve problems? Using momentum. How does a leader create momentum? By helping the team get wins under its belt. If you're not thinking in terms of helping your team win, then you aren't thinking like a Level 3 leader. Find small challenges for individual team members to take on in order to

experience individual wins. Then look for obtainable challenges for people to win together as a team. The greater the number of wins there are both individually and corporately, the more you can increase the difficulty of the challenges. And the more momentum you can gain.

7. **Discern How Team Members Affect Momentum:** Every team has momentum makers, takers, and breakers. As the leader of the team, your job is to know who is who and to lead the team in a way that maximizes the makers, motivates the takers, and minimizes the breakers. Begin by categorizing everyone on the team:

- Momentum Makers (Producers who make things happen):

- Momentum Takers (People who go along for the ride):

- Momentum Breakers (People who cause problems and hurt morale):

Put the majority of time and energy into the momentum makers and place them strategically in the organization so that they make the greatest impact. And enlist their aid to help lead the momentum takers as you motivate them. Meanwhile, have candid conversations with the momentum breakers. Give them a chance to change their attitude and become productive members of the team. However, if they fail to rise up to the challenge, get them off of the team. If that is impossible, then isolate them from the rest of the team to minimize the damage they can do.

8. **Practice the Pareto Principle:** If you want your productivity to be at the highest possible level, then work according to the 80/20 rule. First, focus on your overall efforts. Set aside a block of time to make a list of all of your responsibilities. Then put

them in order of importance according to the impact they make for the good of the organization. You need to make sure the lion's share of your time and effort is focused on the areas at the top of the list. Second, practice the 80/20 rule on a daily basis. Every day list the tasks you must do. Then focus 80 percent of your time on the top 20 percent. Third, focus your team on the top 20 percent. On a regular basis (perhaps daily or weekly), review the team's priorities with them and make sure 80 percent of the team's efforts are focused on the top 20 percent in terms of importance.

9. **Accept Your Role as Change Agent:** Effective leaders on Level 3 take responsibility for making decisions and initiating changes needed for the team to succeed. If you are a leader, accept this responsibility. Be forever on the lookout for ways to improve the team and initiate them. Start today by setting aside an hour to think of five ways to change things for the better. And if things go wrong, take responsibility for that as well.

10. **Don't Neglect Level 2:** There's a lot to be done on Level 3. Because of that, many leaders lose sight of the human element in leadership. As you work on the Production level, don't forget to stay relationally connected to your people. Get out among them and spend time with them. Put connecting times on your schedule, if needed. Do whatever it takes to keep from losing what you've gained on Level 2.

Level 4:
PEOPLE DEVELOPMENT

*Helping Individual Leaders Grow Extends
Your Influence and Impact*

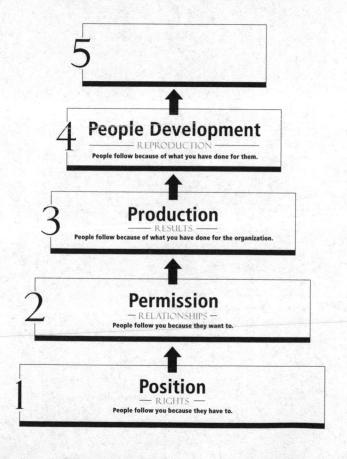

5

4 **People Development**
— REPRODUCTION —
People follow because of what you have done for them.

3 **Production**
— RESULTS —
People follow because of what you have done for the organization.

2 **Permission**
— RELATIONSHIPS —
People follow you because they want to.

1 **Position**
— RIGHTS —
People follow you because they have to.

Effective leaders understand that what got them to their current level of leadership won't be enough to get them to the next one. They understand that if they want to keep getting better as leaders, they have to be willing to keep growing and changing, and that each move up the 5 Levels of Leadership requires a paradigm shift and a change in the way a person leads.

On Level 3, the emphasis is on personal and corporate productivity. The ability to create a high-productivity team, department, or organization indicates a higher level of leadership ability than most others display. But to reach the upper levels of leadership that create elite organizations, leaders must transition from producers to developers. Why? Because people are any organization's most appreciable asset.

> To reach the upper levels of leadership that create elite organizations, leaders must transition from producers to developers.

Good leaders on Level 4 invest their time, energy, money, and thinking into growing others as leaders. They look at every person and try to gauge his or her potential to grow and lead—regardless of the individual's title, position, age, or experience. Every person is a potential candidate for development. This practice of identifying and developing people compounds the positives of their organization, because bringing out the best in a person is often a catalyst for bringing out the best in the team. Developing one person for leadership and success lays the foundation for developing others for success.

> Bringing out the best in a person is often a catalyst for bringing out the best in the team.

Peter Drucker observed,

Making the right people decisions is the ultimate means of controlling an organization well. Such decisions reveal how competent management is, what its values are, and whether it takes its job seriously. No matter how hard managers try to keep their decisions a secret—and some still try hard—people decisions cannot be hidden. They are eminently visible. Executives who do not make the effort to get their people decisions right do more than risk poor performance. They risk losing their organization's respect.[1]

How does this emphasis on people and people decisions translate into action? Leaders on the People Development level of leadership shift their focus from the production achieved by others to the development of their potential. And they put only 20 percent of their focus on their personal productivity while putting 80 percent of it on developing and leading others. This can be a difficult shift for highly productive people who are used to getting their hands dirty, but it's a change that can revolutionize an organization and give it a much brighter future.

The Upside of People Development

The Potential of the Organization Just Got Greater

When you become capable of leading people on Level 4, the upside of leadership becomes even stronger and the potential of the organization increases dramatically. Here are the primary positive benefits of leading on the People Development level:

1. People Development Sets You Apart from Most Leaders

Most leaders are looking for ways to grow their organizations. Where do they usually focus their attention? On Level 3. They work to increase production. That's the wrong focus. How do you grow a company? By growing the people in it. And if you *really* want to expand the organization and its potential, focus on growing the leaders.

Author and friend Denis Waitley once shared with me a wonderful insight about personal development. He said that people need to have the conviction that there is value in their dreams, and he said that it required "the belief that you are worth the effort, time, and energy to develop yourself." That can also be said when it comes to developing others. We must believe in their value. We must value their dreams. We must believe that they are worth the time, effort, energy, and resources that developing them requires. Unfortunately, many leaders do not have that belief.

One of the leaders I admire is Jim Blanchard, for many years the leader of Synovus. In 1999, *Fortune* named the company the best place in America to work. I believe one of the main reasons Synovus was so successful and such a great place to work was because of their dedication to developing people. That started with Blanchard, who said he loved reading books and any kind of opportunity to receive leadership training. Blanchard explained,

> We made a decision twenty-five years ago that…putting people in jobs that they are not prepared for because we have not invested in their training is one mistake we are not going to make.… Training and preparing leaders, teaching them the basics, and trying to enthuse them to seek their own highest level of leadership was a good approach and a good investment in a corporate environment. It has certainly paid off. One thing we learned is that developing leaders is probably the most appreciated benefit in the company. When current or would-be leaders realize that you are investing in their growth, it's more important to them than money. It's more important, in my opinion, than a supervisor taking personal interest in their person and encouraging them along the way in their career, although that is probably second.[2]

That is a good description of the jump from Levels 2 and 3, where a leader builds relationships with people and helps them to be productive in their career, to Level 4, where the leader helps them develop their potential and become the leaders they are capable of being.

> **The mark of someone with potential to grow is openness to the process.**

Blanchard says that the mark of someone

with potential to grow is openness to the process. "When you look at people who are eager to learn more," Blanchard remarked, "you can bet they are on the right track. And when you talk to people who just don't want any more instruction, then they have pretty much hit the wall. They are done."

If you want the best for your organization, you need to invest in its people. That's where the greatest potential is. And in a competitive business world, the ability to develop people is often the difference maker between two organizations competing to succeed using similar resources. Former Secretary of Labor Robert Reich pointed out, "If employers fail to upgrade their workers, then they're trying to be competitive only with their capital. Anybody can replicate physical capital. But the one resource nobody can replicate is the dedication, the teamwork, the skills of a company's employees." Develop them, and you become a one-in-a-thousand leader.

2. People Development Assures That Growth Can Be Sustained

Achieving success isn't easy. Thousands of new businesses are launched every year only to fail a short time later. Those that make it discover that sustaining success isn't easy, either. Many companies said to have been "built to last" don't. Even some of the giants who seem invincible don't remain successful forever. What gives an organization the best chance for sustaining growth and success? Developing and training people. Only by helping your people reach their potential will your organization reach its potential.

In the early years of leadership, I didn't understand this. Equipping and developing others wasn't a high priority for me. Once I discovered the Production level of leadership, that was where I poured my seemingly endless store of energy. I was able to work long hours, and I loved the affirmation that others gave me for my work ethic and productivity.

Words such as "How can you accomplish so much?" were music to my ears. Only after I left an organization did the music stop. I realized that as soon as my personal touch was no longer on a particular task or effort, it wasn't sustained. As a result, many of the things I built ceased to thrive or in some cases even to exist after my exit. I had flunked the leadership test!

This really threw me for a loop. Author and friend Ken Blanchard says, "The test of your leadership is not what happens when you are there, but what happens when you're not there." I wondered what the secret was. Why did some organizations continue to succeed after their leaders left while others fell apart?

I began to gain leadership insight in an unlikely place. One night Margaret and I went to a circus, and in the center ring was a man who began to spin a plate on the end of a stick. (If you're from my generation, you may have seen this done on a variety show.) After he got that first plate spinning, he started to spin another plate on a second stick. Then another and another and another until he had six plates spinning. For the next few minutes he hurried from stick to stick, keeping the plates spinning so that none of them would lose momentum and fall. The more plates spinning, the faster he ran to keep them from falling.

All of a sudden I realized: that was me! I was doing everything myself, and as long as I ran quickly, I could hold everything together. But the moment I stopped, everything would crash around me. By not training anyone else to spin the plates of leadership, I was wearing myself out and limiting the potential of my organization. What a mistake. That was when I made developing others to lead a priority in my organization. It has revolutionized my leadership and made an incredible impact on every organization I've led.

I think many of us come from the paradigm where the leader is connected to everything of importance in an organization. Authors

James A. Belasco and Ralph C. Stayer liken this mind-set to that of a buffalo herd, where everyone waits around to see what the head buffalo thinks and wants to do. Instead, they argue, effective organizations need to be less like herds of buffalo and more like flocks of geese, flying in V formation and sharing the load. Their book *Flight of the Buffalo* states,

> Rather than the old head-buffalo leadership paradigm, I developed a new lead-goose leadership paradigm. Crafted in the crucible of real-time leadership experience, that paradigm is built around the following leadership principles:
>
> - Leaders transfer ownership for work to those who execute the work.
> - Leaders create the environment for ownership where each person wants to be responsible.
> - Leaders coach the development of personal capabilities.
> - Leaders learn fast themselves and encourage others also to learn quickly.[3]

When leaders take this kind of approach, then everyone has the potential to lead—at least in some area and capacity.

If you haven't made developing leaders a priority in the past, allow me to encourage you to do so now. It will take time and commitment, but you can do it. If you have been successful leading on Levels 1, 2, and 3, you have the potential to move up to Level 4. It will require you to shift from doing to developing. It will require you to believe in people. And it will require you to share the load. But if you desire to make the shift in emphasis and put in the work, you can do it. Never forget that leadership is the art of helping people change from who they're thought to be to who they ought to be.

Stephen Covey observes, "People and organizations don't grow much without delegation and completed staff work, because they are confined to the capacities of the boss and reflect both personal strengths and weaknesses." Don't allow yourself to become the lid on your organization. Give it the best chance for a bright future by developing other leaders.

> Don't allow yourself to become the lid on your organization. Give it the best chance for a bright future by developing other leaders.

3. People Development Empowers Others to Fulfill Their Leadership Responsibilities

Many leaders become a lid on their teams or organizations. The typical lid is the person who can't lead yet possesses a leadership position. It's the Peter Principle playing out, where people rise to the level of their incompetence. Because they can't empower and motivate people, their area of responsibility suffers and their people go nowhere. But there is another kind of person who also puts a lid on those he leads: the competent person who won't share responsibility.

People development by its very nature shares responsibility for getting things done. I say that because people development is more than just teaching. It's transforming. It invites people into the process of leadership because many things can be learned only through experience. History provides abundant examples of people whose greatest gift was in redeeming, inspiring, liberating, and nurturing the gifts of others. John Quincy Adams said, "If your actions inspire others to dream more, learn more, do more, and become more, you are a leader." When you give someone responsibility and authority, they not only learn, but they also start to fulfill their leadership responsibilities. That action transforms people and organizations.

When established leaders focus on People Development and empower others to lead, everybody wins. The first benefit comes to the people being led. When new leaders are developed, they become better at what they do and they help everyone who works with them to do the same. When these new leaders start building relationships with their people on Level 2, they treat them better and the working environment improves. When they master Level 3, they become more productive.

The second benefit comes to the organization. With the addition of more good leaders, the organization's current efforts improve. Every developed leader adds more horsepower to the organization. And expanding the leadership of the organization also gives it the ability to expand its territory and take on new initiatives.

The final benefit comes to the leaders who are doing the developing, because new leaders help to share the load. All leaders feel a weight of responsibility for leading. They understand that leaders are expected to produce no matter what. They feel a responsibility to the organization and their leaders to fulfill the vision. If there are stockholders, they feel responsible to them for making a profit. They feel responsible to the people they lead. They want to help them succeed. And they know that people's jobs are ultimately on the line.

One of the principles I teach is that everything rises and falls on leadership. Most people apply that concept to productivity. But it also applies to responsibility. When I owned three companies, I felt the weight of my leadership responsibilities every day. I was responsible for the direction the companies were heading, the values that we were establishing, and the bottom-line success of the organizations. Every leader who has a lot of responsibility in an organization feels that weight. (Anyone who doesn't feel it needs to examine their motives, because they may be taking their responsibility too lightly.)

As you develop people and they begin to share the load of leadership, it's important for you to give them the right expectations. Let them know that you're responsible to them, but not for them. By that I mean you will take responsibility for providing training, supplying tools, offering opportunities, and creating an environment conducive for their development. They must take responsibility for their growth through their choices, attitude, and commitment. If they don't, you will pay for their failure along with them, but that is a risk worth taking because the upside advantages if they succeed are so great. And when it does work and people seize the opportunity to grow and lead, it's fantastic.

Philanthropist Melinda Gates understood this dynamic at an incredibly early age. In her valedictory address at Ursuline Academy in 1982, she said, "If you are successful, it is because somewhere, sometime, someone gave you a life or an idea that started you off in the right direction." That is true for all of us. No leader is self-made. Everyone was given a start by somebody else. That is a gift. Our gift back is to take responsibility and do our best to lead others with effectiveness and integrity.

> "If you are successful, it is because somewhere, sometime, someone gave you a life or an idea that started you off in the right direction."
> —Melinda Gates

Farzin Madjidi, professor of leadership at Pepperdine University, asserts, "We need leaders who empower people and create other leaders. It's no longer good enough for a manager to make sure that everybody has something to do and is producing. Today, all employees must 'buy in' and take ownership of everything they're doing. To foster this, it's important that employees should make decisions that most directly affect them. That's how the best decisions are made. That's the essence of empowerment." What he's describing is Level 4 leadership—leadership that empowers others to share the load. In healthy organizations led by Level 4 leaders, rewards are given for empowering others, not for climbing over them.

If you want to improve an organization, improve its leaders. If you want to grow an organization, grow its leaders. When you increase the number of leaders you have and you make the leaders you have better, the potential of the organization increases greatly.

4. People Development Empowers the Leader to Lead Larger

Many leaders don't want to share responsibility with others because they don't want to lose any of their power. But when you share leadership with others, it doesn't actually take away from you. Instead, it actually gives you something you can get *only* by developing others: it gives you back time. As you develop people and empower them to lead, their territories expand and so does yours. But you are also freed up to do more important things, the most important of which are often thinking, envisioning, and strategizing.

Leaders always need more quality thinking time. Yet because most leaders have a bias toward action, they often don't have it. As you develop other leaders and empower them to lead, they take on work that used to be yours, and you can use that time to take your team or organization to the next level. Everyone benefits.

It's often difficult to hand over responsibility for a task to others, especially if you believe they won't do as good a job as you will. But that's no excuse. You cannot become an effective Level 4 leader unless you are willing to let go of some of your responsibilities. So what's a good rule of thumb for transferring ownership of a leadership responsibility to someone else? I use the 80 percent rule. If someone on my team can do one of my tasks 80 percent as well as I do (or better), then I give him or her responsibility for it. If you want to be an effective leader, you must move from perfectionist to pragmatist.

> If you want to be an effective leader, you must move from perfectionist to pragmatist.

5. People Development Provides
Great Personal Fulfillment

In his book *Man, The Manipulator*, Everett Shostrom quotes a teacher who learned the secret to reaching people and changing their lives:

> I had a great feeling of relief when I began to understand that a youngster needs more than just subject matter. I know mathematics well, and I teach it well. I used to think that was all I needed to do. Now I teach children, not math. I accept the fact that I can only succeed partially with some of them. When I don't have to know all the answers, I seem to have more answers than when I tried to be the expert. The youngster who really made me understand this was Eddie. I asked him one day why he thought he was doing so much better than last year. He gave meaning to my whole new orientation. "It's because I like myself now when I'm with you," he said.[4]

The greatest satisfaction in life comes from giving to others. We are most fulfilled when we forget ourselves and focus on others. And what's really wonderful is that when we add the giving that comes from developing people on Level 4 to the solid relationships we've developed on Level 2, the closeness and warmth that result can provide the richest experiences of our lives. We are often closest to people when we help them grow.

My best friends are the people who have brought out the best in me, and the people I've tried to help be their best. Our growth journey has been filled with laughter and tears, wins and losses, hopes and hurts, questions and answers. I treasure the notes I've received from people who generously share the credit for their growth and success with me.

Howard Schultz, founder of Starbucks, said, "Victory is much more meaningful when it comes not just from one person, but from the joint achievements of many. The euphoria is lasting when all participants lead with their hearts, winning not just for themselves but for one another." That is a good description of how I feel about the people closest to me in life: my family and my inner circle. Just last night I enjoyed dinner with a group of them—all of whom I have developed in some way. We laughed, shared pictures, told stories, and traded ideas. The evening went way too fast.

> "Victory is much more meaningful when it comes not just from one person, but from the joint achievements of many. The euphoria is lasting when all participants lead with their hearts, winning not just for themselves but for one another."
> —*Howard Schultz*

Mark and Stephanie Cole were there. I assisted in their ceremony the day they got married. Now, years later, Mark has become my go-to guy and confidant. Many a project that needs a good leader's attention I give to him. Stephanie freely allows him to travel with me whenever I need him. What a gift. What would I do without them?

David and Lori Hoyt were there. David handles all my speaking engagements with great care and professionalism, representing me so well to so many people. Lori expresses her love and support for me every time I am with her.

Charlie and Stephanie Wetzel were there. Charlie has helped me write for over seventeen years. With over 20 million books sold, I acknowledge that he has become the greatest influencer of others in my inner circle. Stephanie is Ms. Social Media. She manages my blog as well as my Twitter and Facebook accounts. Some in the publishing industry credit her with much of the recent success of my books.

And finally, Patrick and Linda Eggers were there. Patrick used to be a member of my board. He has been a good friend for over thirty years. He's big enough to be my bodyguard and smart enough that he once worked as an honest-to-goodness rocket scientist. Linda has been my assistant for fifteen years. She has been a great friend to my wife, Margaret, and me. Linda knows what I'm thinking before I think it, and she handles everything for us.

As I looked around the table last night, I thought three things: First, these people that I have helped to develop have really grown me. In the beginning I helped them more than they helped me. Today, they help me more than I help them. There is a huge return in developing people!

Second, these are true friends. Our best times are when we are with each other. In 2010, we all went to Israel together and had a blast. The journey of life was not meant to be traveled alone. I'm grateful I get to travel much of it with them.

Third, my greatest fulfillment has come not from the books I have written, the companies I have started, or the recognition I have received. My greatest fulfillment comes from the people I love, and especially from the people whom I have helped to develop.

> "The purpose of life is not to win. The purpose of life is to grow and to share. When you come to look back on all that you have done in life, you will get more satisfaction from the pleasures you have brought into other people's lives than you will from the times that you outdid and defeated them."
> —*Harold Kushner*

Rabbi Harold Kushner asserted, "The purpose of life is not to win. The purpose of life is to grow and to share. When you come to look back on all that you have done in life, you will get more satisfaction from the pleasures you have brought into other people's lives than you will from the times that you outdid and defeated them." That is great wisdom. Helping others grow and develop brings great joy, satisfaction, and energy to a leader. If you can achieve Level 4 as a leader, you will create a sense of community where victories are celebrated, gratitude is evident, and loyalty is shared. Level 4 is the sweetest of all levels a leader can achieve.

The Downside of People Development

Leading on Level 4 Requires High Levels of Maturity and Skill

There is a reason that many leaders don't develop people. It's not easy! And there's no guarantee that it will work out. Every leader has horror stories of investment in others that turned out badly. You pour yourself into some people and nothing happens. Some people take without giving anything in return. Others make an effort but fall far short of your expectations. And sometimes you give your best to someone, he turns out to be an absolute star, and then he leaves and becomes part of another organization! What can be worse than that? Well, how about not training them and having them stay? If you think about it, you have only one great choice as a leader if you want to lead to the full extent of your potential; you need to invest in your people.

People development requires a very high maturity level. It also requires a very high level of skill. That can create problems for some leaders, and it prevents many from following through with it. Here are the primary causes of breakdowns on Level 4:

1. Self-Centeredness Can Cause Leaders to Neglect People Development

Maturity is the ability to think beyond yourself, see things from the perspective of others, and place their needs above your own. Selfishness prevents people from reaching that level of maturity.

My friend Gerald Brooks says, "When you become a leader you give up the right to think about yourself." Becoming a Level 4 leader requires us to recognize that we now have the authority to serve people in a special way and we need to exercise that ability. You can't do that if you have a self-serving attitude.

> "When you become a leader you give up the right to think about yourself."
> —Gerald Brooks

If you want to lead on Level 4, you need to focus 80 percent of your attention on others and helping them to grow, learn, and achieve. If your focus is always on yourself and what you want, then people become an obstacle to your goals. *Their* needs are seen as interfering with *your* goals. And you spend most of your time disappointed with others because they aren't on your selfish agenda and are forever letting you down.

Leadership expert and author Max Depree says, "The leader is the servant who removes the obstacles that prevent people from doing their jobs." What a great description. That kind of Level 4 mind-set requires maturity. It means coming to work every day placing other people first in our thoughts and actions. It means asking, "Who can I add value to today?" and "What can I do for others?" That is not the mind-set of an immature leader. It is the mindset of a People Developer.

> "The leader is the servant who removes the obstacles that prevent people from doing their jobs."
> —Max Depree

So if you want to move up to Level 4 leadership, get over your selfishness, get outside of yourself, and adopt the attitude of speaker and master salesman Zig Ziglar, who said, "If you will help others get what they want, they will help you get what you want."

2. Insecurity Can Make Leaders Feel Threatened by People Development

My friend Wayne Schmidt, vice president of Wesley Seminary at Indiana Wesleyan University, once told me, "No amount of personal competency can compensate for personal insecurity." He is so right. Insecure leaders continually sabotage themselves and others. And because they worry about their position and standing, they have a hard time investing in other people.

> "No amount of personal competency can compensate for personal insecurity."
> —*Wayne Schmidt*

Why? Because they fear that someone will take their place. For that reason, leaders who don't deal with their insecurities and overcome them rarely reach Level 4 as leaders.

If you suspect that your insecurities may prevent you from moving up to the People Development level of leadership, then be prepared to do some work in the following three areas:

Ego

Leaders who are honest with themselves know that they don't have all the answers. They recognize that success always comes from the combined contributions of everyone on a team. Success comes when people work together, each person playing his or her part. And because of this, they don't try to answer every question themselves. They don't try to make every decision. They see winning as a collaborative effort. And their goal isn't to make others think more highly of them. It's to get their people to think more highly of themselves.

How can you tell if your ego might be getting in the way of your ability to move up to Level 4? Consider what happens when you meet with your team.

- Do your team members share their thoughts and ideas freely?
- Are the best ideas rarely your ideas?
- If you often contribute ideas, does the discussion quickly move from your idea to the best idea—and you're happy about it?

How about when your team performs?

- When your team succeeds, do the other team members get the majority of the credit?
- Is there a shared sense of pride in the work that's being done?
- When things go wrong, do you personally accept the greatest share of the blame?

If you can honestly answer yes to these questions, ego may not be a problem. If you answered no to many of those questions, beware. You may need to deal with your ego. Positive working environments led by secure leaders allow team members to get the credit. Level 4 leaders experience genuine joy in the success of others. When others shine, so do they.

Control

Author Tom Peters observed, "There is nothing more useless than the person who says at the end of the day, 'Well, I made it through the day without screwing up.'" Why would anyone have that kind of goal? Because they're afraid of making mistakes. Many insecure workers try to avoid making mistakes by doing as little as possible or by trying to keep a low profile. Insecure leaders often deal with the issue differently. They rely on control. They think if they micromanage their people, they can keep them from making mistakes.

Unfortunately, controlling leaders don't understand that progress comes only from taking risks and making mistakes. They would be better off taking the advice of someone like Chuck Braun, of Idea Connections Systems, who developed the concept of the "Mistake Quota." When he trains people, he tells students that he expects them to make thirty mistakes per training session. Braun says he can almost hear the sighs of relief in the room as people relax and begin participating.

Good leaders forge ahead, break ground, and make mistakes. And they expect the same from their people. Authors James M. Kouzes and Barry Z. Posner say it this way: "Leaders are pioneers—people who are willing to step out into the unknown. They are people who are willing to take risks, to innovate and experiment in order to find new and better ways of doing things." To succeed as a leader on Level 4, you must embrace that attitude and give up controlling others.

Since you can't prevent mistakes, why not adopt an attitude in which you and your team learn from them? That's the only way anyone can really profit from mistakes anyway. So don't try to put people in a box. Try to help them make the most of their fumbles, flops, and failures. As Jack Welch, the former CEO of General Electric, said, "A leader's role is not to control people or stay on top of things,

> "A leader's role is not to control people or stay on top of things, but rather to guide, energize, and excite."
> —*Jack Welch*

but rather to guide, energize, and excite." That's what Level 4 leaders do.

Trust

Different leaders see trust in different ways. Secure leaders see it as the glue that keeps relationships together and makes business work. Stephen M. R. Covey, author of *The Speed of Trust,* says that trust produces speed because it feeds collaboration, loyalty, and, ultimately, results. Contrast that with the words of Al Neuharth, former CEO of the U.S. newspaper chain Gannett and author of *Confessions of an S.O.B.* He wrote, "Now that I was on top, I knew others would want to topple me...I believe in practicing the S.O.B.'s Golden Rule: *Expect others to do unto you what you would do to them.*" I don't know about you, but I don't want to live with that kind of attitude.

Insecure leaders don't place their trust in others, nor do they engender trust from others. As a result, they don't invest in others. And they don't become Level 4 leaders. As a leader, you should never take trust for granted. Only when you lose it do you really understand the value of it. My daughter Elizabeth learned this in high school when she was a cheerleader. Because Elizabeth was tiny, she was a flyer. That means she was always either at the top of their pyramid or being tossed high into the air. With daredevil abandonment she would soar. How was she able to take such risks? Trust. She had practiced with her teammates for hours, having been thrown and safely caught hundreds of times. Then during her senior year, an inattentive teammate missed and let her fall on a throw. She wasn't the same after that. From then on, she experienced moments of hesitation whenever she was thrown.

If you want to become a People Development leader, you must give others your trust and earn their trust in return. There is no other way to succeed on Level 4.

3. Shortsightedness Can Keep Leaders from Seeing the Need for People Development

How many times have you considered giving someone something to do and instead thought, *It's easier to just do it myself?* I bet you've done it often. Why? Because it *is* easier. Doing work yourself is always faster and easier than developing other people to do it. But that's short-term thinking! To become a developer of people, you have to

> To become a developer of people, you have to be willing to adopt a long-term mind-set.

be willing to adopt a long-term mind-set. If you pay the price on the front end, the return is great on the back end. On Level 4, the question isn't "What can you do?" The question is "Who can you develop?" Investing in people takes a lot of time and energy.

Shortsightedness, like selfishness and insecurity, is another sign of immaturity in a leader. People Development requires big-picture thinking. It takes patience. Helping another person to become a competent leader almost always takes longer than you think and is more difficult than you expect. You must do it anyway. Otherwise you limit the potential for yourself, your people, and your organization.

4. Lack of Commitment Can Keep Leaders from Doing the Hard Work of People Development

Nearly anyone can lead others positionally. Many people can lead others relationally. Few people can be productive and put a team together to achieve goals. But very few people are both able and willing to develop others to become leaders. That is why most leaders only ever lead followers. Anyone who can relate well with people, produce personally, and communicate a vision is capable of attracting a following. However, attracting, developing, and leading other leaders is much more difficult. And most leaders are not willing to put forth the tremendous effort it takes and to make the sacrifices necessary to do it.

In the organizations I have led, developing people has been a high priority. I tell the leaders who work for me, "Your job is to work yourself out of your job." By that I mean that I want leaders to figure out how to do the job with the highest level of excellence, recruit a team, develop them, model leadership, find a potential successor, train and develop that person, and empower him or her to lead in their place. When people do that, they've worked themselves out of a job, and they're ready to move up to the next job.

That's a high bar of expectation for leaders. In some organizations, leaders can't even get the job done on their own, much less develop some-one else to do it. But that's what Level 4 leadership takes. In my world of leadership, People Development is the target for every leader I employ. And if they are not willing or able to work themselves out of their job, I might have to take the job away from them and give it to someone else who can. So the goal for my leaders is never to keep their jobs. The ques-tion to them is, "Will you lose it by developing others or will you lose it because you didn't develop others?" It's always the leader's choice.

My nonprofit organization EQUIP exists to help leaders in countries around the world develop people to lead on Level 4. Every six months EQUIP sends two associate trainers to a site to train leaders. For two days they take indigenous leaders through training material in a conference setting, equipping them for leadership. At the end of the conference, these leaders are given training materials in their own language that they can take back and use to train potential leaders in their sphere of influence. They are also given additional books to help them continue growing dur-ing those six months between sessions with EQUIP's associate trainers. As long as these local leaders are committed to training their own people and becoming Level 4 leaders themselves, they are welcome to engage in EQUIP's training process. In this way, EQUIP has been able to train mil-lions of leaders internationally during the past decade.

In many countries where EQUIP works, this concept at first seems odd to people. Many leaders, especially in developing nations, are very positional and territorial. Their goal is to obtain a position of power, attract as many followers as they can, and do whatever is necessary to hold on to their power. The idea of giving themselves away by develop-ing and empowering others to lead is very counterintuitive. But many get it. They do it. And they see the incredible impact People Develop-ment can make. It transforms organizations and even impacts cultures. But it takes a high level of security and skill to do. And it requires a high degree of commitment.

Best Behaviors on Level 4

How to Develop People

Only leaders can develop other people to become leaders. A well-intentioned person with no leadership knowledge and experience cannot train another person to lead. Theorists who study leadership without practicing it cannot equip someone to lead, no more than a cookbook reader who has no experience in the kitchen would be able to teach someone how to cook. Nobody really understands leadership until he or she does it. Put another way...

It Takes a Leader to KNOW a Leader (Recruiting and Positioning)
It Takes a Leader to SHOW a Leader (Modeling and Equipping)
It Takes a Leader to GROW a Leader (Developing, Empowering, and Measuring)

In light of that truth, my goal in this section on People Development is to give you a clear path to follow as you seek to develop other people to lead. My assumption going into this is that you are already leading people somewhere in some fashion. If you are (or have in the past), the following seven steps will make sense. If not, you will need to gain experience leading on Levels 1, 2, and 3 before you will be capable of implementing these Level 4 best behaviors.

> Only leaders can develop other people to become leaders.

If you want to make the most of People Development and raise up others to lead, then follow these guidelines:

1. Recruiting—Find the Best People Possible

Recruiting is the first and most important task in developing people and creating winning organizations. College football coach Bobby Bowden says, "If you get the best players and coach them soundly, you're going to win." In college sports, the most successful coaches

> "If you get the best players and coach them soundly, you're going to win."
> —Bobby Bowden

are the ones who are the best recruiters. You can't develop people without potential—no matter how hard you work at it. So the people you recruit must possess natural ability in the area where they are to be developed, exhibit the desire to grow, and be a good fit for the organization.

The key to success in recruiting is a clear picture of who you are looking for. Many years ago Charlie Grimm was the manager of Major League Baseball's Chicago Cubs. Speaker Linda Ellerbee tells the story of how one season the Cubs were having a hard time winning games because they didn't have any good hitters. It's said that Grimm received a phone call one day from an excited scout, who enthused, "Charlie, I've landed the greatest young pitcher in the land. He struck out every man who came to bat. Twenty-seven in a row. Nobody even got a foul until two were out in the ninth. The pitcher is right here with me. What shall I do?"

"Sign up the guy who got the foul," answered Grimm. "We're looking for hitters."

This may sound overly simplistic, but it's true nonetheless: it's easier to find something when you know what you're looking for. Say you're looking for a tool on a messy workbench. If you know what it looks like, you can find it much more quickly and easily than if you don't. If you're trying to find a can in your pantry, you can find it more quickly and easily if you know what color and size it is.

It's the same for potential leaders. If you know what you're looking for, your chance of finding them goes up astronomically. Recruiting a nonleader to be developed in leadership is like asking a horse to climb a tree. It just isn't going to happen. If you want a potential tree climber, find a squirrel. If you want a potential leader, find someone with the traits of a good leader.

When I go looking for potential leaders, I use what I call the Four Cs:

Chemistry

Let's begin with the easiest one: it doesn't take long to figure out if you like people who are applying for a job or asking to be mentored. Is liking them important? Absolutely. If you don't like the person, you will not be an effective mentor to them. It's very difficult to spend time with people, be open with them, and invest in them if you don't like them and want to be around them.

If you are seriously considering recruiting or promoting someone, ask members of your team to spend time with that individual, preferably in a social setting if possible. After they've been around the person, find out if your team likes and would enjoy working with him or her. If not, there may not be a good fit. The Friendship Principle, which I describe in my book *Winning with People*, always applies: "All things being equal, people will work with people they like; all things not being equal, they still will." Chemistry matters.

Character

Good character makes trust possible. Trust makes strong relationships possible. Strong relationships make mentoring possible. You won't be able to develop someone whose character you do not trust.

> Good character makes trust possible. Trust makes strong relationships possible. Strong relationships make mentoring possible.

Character is what closes the gap between knowing and doing. It aligns intentions and action. That consistency is appealing, and it is also essential to good, credible leadership. If I suspect that someone I'm considering recruiting doesn't have strong character, I don't go through with it.

Jim Rohn observed, "Good people are found, not changed." He said that he came across a slogan from a company stating, "We don't teach people to be nice. We simply hire

> "Good people are found, not changed."
> —Jim Rohn

nice people." He thought that was a clever shortcut. It's also good leadership. If you go into a mentoring relationship expecting to change a person's character, you're liable to be disappointed.

Capacity

During the NBA playoffs, I heard commentator and former player Charles Barkley distinguish the difference between a star player and a support player. "The stars can *at any time* meet the requirements needed to help the team," explained Barkley. "Support players can *sometimes* do that." (Emphases mine.) What determines the difference between these two types of players? Capacity.

Fulfillment on Level 4 is bringing out the best in people. Frustration is trying to bring out what isn't there. If you want to develop people and help them become good leaders, you must not ask for what they *wish* they could give, only for what they have the potential to give. I haven't always found it easy to assess other people's capacity. It was especially difficult for me when I began my leadership career. But with experience I began to see patterns in people.

As you look at potential leaders, try to assess their capacity in the following areas:

- Stress Management—their ability to withstand and overcome pressure, failure, deadlines, and obstacles
- Skill—their ability to get specific tasks done
- Thinking—their ability to be creative, develop strategy, solve problems, and adapt
- Leadership—their ability to gather followers and build a team
- Attitude—their ability to remain positive and tenacious amidst negative circumstances

As a leader, your goal should be to identify what their capacity is, recognize what *they* think their capacity is, and motivate, challenge, and equip them in such a way that they close the gap between the two.

Contribution

Some people possess an X factor. They are winners. They contribute beyond their job responsibilities, and they lift the performance of everyone on their team. When you discover people with these characteristics, recruit them. They are a joy to develop, and whatever you put into them returns to you compounded.

One such person in my life is Mark Cole, whom I mentioned previously. He has been working with me for twelve years and has a track record of making everything he touches better. Everyone who works with him performs better as a result of his contact. It has been a joy to develop him because of his servant's heart and superior skills. What a combination!

Once when I was having lunch with coach Lou Holtz, he told me with a grin, "I've had good players and I've had bad players. I'm a better coach with good players." The same is true with leaders. If you want to be better, recruit better

> "I've had good players and I've had bad players. I'm a better coach with good players."
> —*Lou Holtz*

players. If you want to develop better leaders, recruit people with potential according to the Four Cs.

2. Positioning—Placing the Right People in the Right Position

Red Auerbach won nine NBA championships as coach of the Boston Celtics and sixteen championships overall as coach, general manager, and front office president. Few leaders in sports have come anywhere close to his accomplishments. Once, when asked about his team's success, Auerbach said,

> When I first started coaching, people told me to put my five best players on the court. But I learned early on that this was not the key to success. It wasn't putting the five best players on the court that was going to cause us to win. It was putting the five players on the court *who could work together the best*. We won championships because we put people together. They weren't always our best players.

In other words, it's not enough just to recruit good players. A leader must understand how those players best fit on the team and put them there. To do that, he must have a clear picture of each person's strengths and weakness and understand how they fit the needs of the team.

Author Jim Collins has helped many of us to understand this principle. In his book *Good to Great*, he writes about the importance of getting the right people in the right seats on the bus. Successful people find their right seats. Successful leaders help their people find their right seats. Sometimes that requires moving people around to find where they make the greatest contribution. Sometimes it means trying and failing. As a leader, you have to take it all in stride. Positioning people correctly is a process, and you have to treat it that way. But if you don't do it, you will never help your people reach their potential, nor will you create a team of championship caliber, as Red Auerbach did.

3. Modeling—Showing Others How to Lead

I once read a story about a woman who took her young son to see Indian leader Mahatma Gandhi. "Mahatma," she requested, "please tell my little boy to stop eating sugar."

"Come back in three days," said Gandhi.

Three days passed and the woman returned with her son.

"Young boy, stop eating sweets. They are not good for you," Gandhi said to the little boy.

Puzzled, the woman asked, "Why did you ask us to leave and come back in three days? I don't understand."

"I asked you to return with the boy in three days," replied the leader, "because three days ago, I, too, was eating sweets. I could not ask him to stop eating sweets so long as I had not stopped eating sweets"[5]

I've already written about how important it is to model what you want to see in others, so I won't say a lot more about it here. However, as I think about developing others, here are the things I believe I must model with integrity in order to help people to develop on Level 4:

Authenticity—This is the foundation for developing people.
Servanthood—This is the soul for developing people.
Growth—This is the measurement for developing people.
Excellence—This is the standard for developing people.
Passion—This is the fuel for developing people.
Success—This is the purpose for developing people.

And allow me to mention one more thing: When discussing Level 3, where you focus on Production, I mentioned how important it is not to neglect Level 2 relationships. Similarly, when focusing on Level 4 People Development, do not neglect the modeling that you worked to establish on Level 3.

4. Equipping—Helping Others Do Their Jobs Well

Comedian Jack Benny was once appointed as honorary manager of the Hollywood All-Stars baseball team. As the team prepared to play an exhibition game against a professional team in Los Angeles, Jack handed a bat to his first batter and said, "Go up to the plate and hit a home run."

The batter struck out, and with great theatrics, Jack Benny quit as manager. "How can I manage them," he quipped, "if they won't follow orders?"

It's not enough to simply tell people what they need to do. That's not developing their potential. Instead, a leader must *help* them to do their jobs and do them well. Peter Drucker pointed out, "The largest single source of failed promotion is the failure to think through and help others to think through what a new job requires."

> "The largest single source of failed promotion is the failure to think through and help others to think through what a new job requires."
> —*Peter Drucker*

How does a leader equip people to do their work and succeed at it? The best method I've ever found is a five-step equipping process. Here's how it works:

Step 1—I do it (competence).

Step 2—I do it and you are with me (demonstration).

Step 3—You do it and I am with you (coaching).

Step 4—You do it (empowerment).

Step 5—You do it and someone is with you (reproduction).

If you adopt this method, not only will you equip leaders, you will begin teaching them how to equip others, which sets them up to become Level 4 leaders themselves.

5. Developing—Teaching Them to Do Life Well

One of the recurring things I hear from leaders in America who work with people in their twenties is how talented they are—and how few life skills they possess. Some speculate that this generation's struggle to navigate the basics of life is due to the breakdown of the family and the absence of strong fathers in the home. No matter what the cause may be, it is the responsibility of a leader on Level 4 to help people to learn how to do life well. If the only thing you're helping a new leader learn is how to get ahead in the workplace, you're not truly developing that person to succeed, because there's a lot more to life than work and career.

The Greek philosopher Socrates said, "The individual leads in order that those who are led can develop their potential as human beings and thereby prosper." That should be your goal in developing people.

> "The individual leads in order that those who are led can develop their potential as human beings and thereby prosper."
> —*Socrates*

The Center for Creative Leadership has observed that three key elements drive leadership development in others: assessment, challenge, and support. What do these things mean to you as a developing leader?

Assessment

As a Level 4 leader, you should be continually on the lookout for holes in the life skills of someone you are leading and developing. Ask yourself:

Where does this person seem to be failing?

Where are this person's blind spots?

What does my intuition tell me is "off" in this person's thinking?

Why isn't this person reaching his or her potential?

Who is this person following who might be leading him or her in a wrong direction?

When does this person do well?

When does this person stumble?

What telltale clues can I find that give me insight into where this person needs help?

Where is this person's sweet spot?

A good Level 4 leader is always on the lookout for a person's weaknesses and wrong thinking—not to exploit that person, but to strengthen and help him or her succeed.

Challenge

If you've done your work on Level 2 to build a strong relationship with the people, and you've proven yourself on Level 3 by modeling success and productivity, there is a very good chance that they will buy into your leadership and accept a challenge from you to improve. To do that, ask the people you lead to do the following:

Read books related to their areas of strength.

Attend conferences that will inspire them.

Take on new and challenging tasks in their sweet spot.

Practice difficult disciplines that slowly build character.

Meet with you on a regular basis for mentoring.

The idea is to challenge them in every area of their lives where you see that they need improvement. Just be sure to gain their permission to do it before starting the process.

Support

Nobody gets ahead in life without the help and support of other people. One of the great privileges of leading on the People Development level is helping new leaders navigate through life's difficulties. The primary way I do that is by allowing the people I mentor to request a meeting with me whenever they need it. On those occasions, they are to drive the agenda by asking specific, difficult questions. I answer them as best I can, and in return, the next time we meet, I ask that the person tell me how they applied what they learned.

It's difficult for someone to make the most of their leadership potential when the rest of their life is a wreck. Good life skills help a person to create a strong foundation upon which to build a family, career, and spiritual life. I admit that I get the greatest joy from seeing people reach their leadership potential, but it is also very satisfying to know that I've helped someone to enjoy life and live it well.

6. Empowering—Enabling People to Succeed

President Theodore Roosevelt is often quoted as saying, "The best executive is the one who has sense enough to pick good men to do what he wants done, and self-restraint enough to keep from meddling with them while they do it." What he's describing is empowerment. That's helping people to see what they can do without your help, and releasing them to do it.

I have to admit that as a leader, it's hard not to meddle. That's especially true when you know the work you're delegating very well but the person you're giving it to is new to it. Yet releasing work to be done by others is an essential link to empowering and ultimately developing them as leaders.

As you release tasks to the leaders you're developing, you need to trust them, believe in them, and hold them accountable. Trust creates a bond between you and them. When I trust the people I will empower, I put a little piece of myself into their hands. When they respond in kind, the shared vulnerability creates a bond between you that deepens the relationship.

> When I trust the people I will empower, I put a little piece of myself into their hands.

When you believe in people, you motivate them. Few things put wind in another person's sails like your faith in them. And the belief must be genuine. Pretending you believe provides no passion for empowerment. Nor can you borrow the belief from someone else because it will have no power. You must draw upon the experiences you have with them and the growth that they have already exhibited. Besides helping them, it will also help you. If you don't believe in them, you won't be able to let go and release them to achieve.

When you hold people accountable, you increase their chances for positive results. Why? Because everyone finds focus in goals. They work better toward deadlines. And they usually rise to the level of a leader's expectations. Without accountability, people drift. With it, they achieve results.

7. Measuring—Evaluating Those Whom You Develop to Maximize Their Efforts

Many people look at winning sports teams, and they often tend to attribute the team's success to how knowledgeable the coach is. But games aren't won according to what the coach knows. Games are won according to what the coach's players have learned. How can you measure that as a leader? By judging how independently your team members are able to function.

The Center for Organizational Effectiveness in Cincinnati, Ohio, suggests that there are different degrees of ability when it comes to empowerment, based on how independently a team member can work.

Here are the six they recognize, from least independent to most independent:

1. Look into it. Report. I'll decide what to do.
2. Look into it. Report alternatives with pros and cons and your recommendation.
3. Look into it. Let me know what you intend to do, but don't do it unless I say yes.
4. Look into it. Let me know what you intend to do and do it unless I say no.
5. Take action. Let me know what you did.
6. Take action. No further contact required.

As you work in People Development with team members, you can measure where they are in leadership development based on where they typically function according to those six benchmarks. Obviously, your goal is to help them become leaders who can take action without needing your input. When the leaders you develop reach that benchmark, then they—and you—are ready to lead them at the highest level of leadership, Level 5, which I'll discuss in the final section of this book.

The Laws of Leadership at the People Development Level

As you work to master the People Development level of leadership, please keep in mind how the following Laws of Leadership come into play.

The Law of Process
Leadership Develops Daily, Not in a Day

No matter how much you want to be a good leader, it will take you time to improve your leadership. Leadership develops daily, not in a day. Likewise, developing people also takes time. You can't make it happen using a "microwave" mind-set. You have to be willing to take it step by step. You have to put in many hours of mentoring and wait months, years, and sometimes decades for people to develop into good leaders. But it's worth the effort. Just remember: mentoring is not a race. If you run fast and try to finish first, you'll finish alone. Leaders who make it to Level 4 cross the finish line in the company of the people they've developed.

> Mentoring is not a race. If you run fast and try to finish first, you'll finish alone.

The Law of Addition
Leaders Add Value by Serving Others

As a young leader I thought, *It will be great to have people follow me toward my vision and help me achieve it.* I could hardly wait for others to put me first in their lives. I was leading for all the wrong reasons. Good leaders put their people first, not themselves.

If you want to become a great leader, serve the people you lead. Make their success your success. Clear the way for them to achieve. Invest in them so that they succeed. Maintain the mind-set of a servant. Many people pursue success. Few pursue success for their people.

The Law of the Inner Circle
A Leader's Potential Is Determined by Those Closest to Him

The highest levels of achievement in life cannot be accomplished by any person working alone. People need one another. If you are a leader with a big vision, you won't be able to achieve it without a team of leaders—an inner circle. These people help you lead and achieve, and are almost like an extended family. If you desire to have a great inner circle, then start developing people. Only by raising up leaders and inviting them to pursue the vision with you will you achieve big things.

> **"The first method of estimating the intelligence of a ruler is to look at the men he has around him."**
> **—*Niccolo Machiavelli***

Niccolo Machiavelli said, "The first method of estimating the intelligence of a ruler is to look at the men he has around him." Look at the people closest to you. What is their caliber? What can be said about their integrity? A leader's inner circle is the most accurate picture of his or her life. If you don't like what you see, then invest more of yourself into potential leaders and raise them up to succeed. They in turn will do the same for you.

The Law of Empowerment
Only Secure Leaders Give Power to Others

I once heard Jack Welch say in an interview that when he was at GE, he noticed there were two types of leaders: those who would hide their key players and those who would promote them. He said the leaders who hid their best people had a selfish spirit. In contrast, those who promoted and empowered others had a generous spirit.

People don't reach Level 4 unless they are willing to empower leaders, promote them, and release them to lead. That takes a strong sense of security and an abundance mind-set. If you want to succeed on the People Development level of leadership, work to address your insecurities so that you can become an empowerer of other leaders.

The Law of Explosive Growth
To Add Growth, Lead Followers—
To Multiply, Lead Leaders

Leadership productivity and organizational impact begin to occur when a leader reaches Level 3. Those things multiply on Level 4. Every time you develop people and help them become leaders, you not only gain their ability and put their horsepower to use in the organization, but you also engage the abilities of everyone they lead. There is not a faster or more effective way to compound your time, effort, and resources than by developing leaders.

The Law of Buy-In
People Buy into the Leader, Then the Vision

You may have noticed that this is the third time I've referenced the Law of Buy-In. Why? Because developing influence with others is a continuing process of earning their buy in.

Few things are more inspiring and energizing than leaders who seek to serve their people and see those people rise up to their potential and become leaders themselves. When leaders act worthy of their positions on Level 1, build good relationships on Level 2, model productivity on Level 3, and invest in their people by developing them on Level 4, people go beyond just knowing the vision. They feel the vision. Why? Because it comes to life in the leader. People find that inspiring and energizing. And they buy in.

Beliefs That Help a Leader
Move Up to Level 5

If you have managed to move up to Level 4, you are leading at a very high level, higher than 90 percent of all other leaders. But there is still one level higher that may be within your reach. Fewer than 1 percent of all leaders achieve it. To prepare yourself to attempt that final climb and give yourself the best chance of making it to the top, you must first embrace the following beliefs:

1. The Highest Goal of Leadership Is to Develop Leaders, Not Gain Followers or Do Work

Getting work done can be important and rewarding. And leading others and having them help you achieve a vision can be wonderful. But developing others is even more wonderful. And it should be your goal as a leader.

I believe I've already made a pretty good case for how leaders become more productive by focusing on leadership development. But I think it is worth saying that the improvement to individual leaders' lives is the highest goal of leadership development. When you help other people become leaders, you change their lives. You change the way they see the world. You change their capacity. You increase their potential. You change the way they

> The improvement to individual leaders' lives is the highest goal of leadership development.

interact with others. If they become good leaders, you help them improve not only their lives, but also the lives of everyone they touch. I believe that is how you change the world for the better.

How does a leader do this? By applying the Pareto Principle. I described in Level 3 how the 80/20 rule can be used to increase productivity. That same principle can be used when developing leaders. As a Level 4 leader, you should focus 80 percent of your attention on developing the best 20 percent of the leaders you have. That focus will bring you the highest return. A handful of leaders will give an organization a far greater return than hundreds of followers.

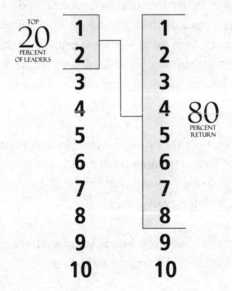

Focusing your development on the top 20 percent also sets you up for success on Level 5 because the leaders with the most potential and who give you the highest rate of return on your investment also have the greatest likelihood of turning around and raising up other leaders, which is the emphasis on Level 5.

2. To Develop Leaders, You Must Create a Leadership Culture

Even if you place great emphasis on developing leaders and practice the 80/20 rule, you will not be able to move up to Level 5 unless you also create a leadership culture. Jim Blanchard did this at Synovus. In an interview with George Barna, Blanchard said, "I think the most important and difficult thing is to create a culture in the organization where leadership is really important. It's important for people in the company to realize that this is a growth-oriented company, and the biggest thing we have to grow here is you, because it's you who will make this company better by your own growth.... So I would think making a culture aware of the significance of developing leaders is valuable." Blanchard went on to ask some critical questions that help leaders examine whether they are indeed working to create a leadership culture and putting the right emphasis on developing leaders. He asked,

> What percentage of the payroll goes into leadership development?
> What kinds of formal training do they do?
> To what extent do they reward leadership?
> Do they have a directory of good mentors?[6]

If you want to start creating a Leadership Development culture that cultivates Level 5 leaders, then do the following:

Champion Leadership —Define and model good leadership.

Teach Leadership— Train leaders on a regular, frequent, consistent basis.

Practice Leadership—Help emerging leaders to plan and execute, fail and succeed.

Coach Leadership—Review new leaders' performance and correct their errors.

Reward Leadership—Reward good leadership with pay, resources, and recognition.

If you make the purpose of your organization to champion, teach, practice, coach, and reward leadership, then people will want to become good leaders. They will strive to help others become good leaders. And the potential of the organization to fulfill its vision will explode.

3. Developing Leaders Is a Life Commitment, Not a Job Commitment

Level 4 leaders develop people. Level 5 leaders consistently develop leaders over a lifetime, and the leaders they raise up also develop leaders. It becomes a lifestyle they practice everywhere and at all times, not a program they implement or a task they occasionally practice. Mentoring is a mantle that they wear willingly, and they strive to add value to others. They value it because they have transitioned from chasing a position of success to pursuing a role of significance.

We live in a very needy world. If you often ask yourself, *How do we meet so many needs?* then please realize that the greatest needs will never be met until we equip leaders who can work to meet those needs. That is one of the reasons I train leaders. I believe it is a cause worthy of a lifetime commitment. I hope you will accept the challenge to develop people and raise up leaders. If you do, you won't regret it.

Guide to Growing through Level 4

As you reflect on the upsides, downsides, best behaviors, and beliefs related to the People Development level of leadership, use the following guidelines to help you grow as a leader:

1. **Be Willing to Keep Growing Yourself:** Few things are worse than the teacher who is unteachable. As a leader, you will reproduce what you are. If you remain teachable, your people will remain teachable. If your mind is closed, so will be the minds of the people you mentor. How do you keep growing and have an open mind? First, maintain a teachable spirit, which says, *Everyone can teach me something. Everything can teach me something.* Second, keep yourself on a growth plan. It is impossible to help others intentionally grow if you are not intentionally growing. And here's the good news: If you have already been investing in your personal development, guess what? You have already done much of the hard work. Just keep learning.

> **Few things are worse than the teacher who is unteachable.**

2. **Decide that People Are Worth the Effort:** Comedian and author David Sedaris said, "I haven't got the slightest idea how to change people, but still I keep a long list of prospective candidates just in case I should ever figure it out."[7] That's not the

way to approach People Development. You shouldn't go into it because people cause trouble and you want them to change. You should go into it because people are worth it, and you're willing to take the trouble to help them. If you haven't already made that decision, then make it before you engage in the process.

> "I haven't got the slightest idea how to change people, but I keep a long list of prospective candidates just in case I should ever figure it out."
> —*David Sedaris*

3. **Work Through Your Insecurities:** Leaders who are afraid of looking bad or of being replaced rarely develop other leaders. If that description applies to you, then you need to process through those issues so that you can work your way up to the higher levels of leadership. Spend some time with people you trust and who know you well enough to talk through your issues. Ask for their help and accountability. Get the advice of a counseling professional, if needed. Do whatever it takes, because insecure leaders don't develop people, and leaders who don't develop people never become Level 4 leaders.

4. **Recruit the Best People You Can to Develop:** Most leaders spend their time and energy on the wrong people: the bottom 20 percent. The individuals who usually take up most of a leader's time are the troublemakers, the complainers, and those who are struggling. These people often have the *least* potential to lead and take the organization forward. Level 4 leaders focus their best time and energy on the top 20 percent, the people who don't *need* attention but would most profit from it. Take a look at all of the people in your sphere of influence. Who are the individuals with the greatest potential to lead and make an impact? These are the people to target for development.

5. **Commit to Spend the Time Needed to Develop Leaders:**
   People development takes a lot of time. To lead on Level 4, you
   may need to dedicate as much as half of your time to developing people if you want to properly invest in them. In order to do
   that, first build a support system to free yourself up; when you
   have to do everything yourself, you have little time to mentor
   others. Second, determine the amount of time you give someone based on his or her potential. A leader's value is in the
   investment he makes in others, not in what he can do personally. That investment must be made wisely and should be a top
   priority.

6. **Create a Personal Development Process:** Benjamin Franklin
   observed, "The eye of the master will do more work than both
   his hands." The ability to see, discern, and analyze is essential
   to developing people. Level 4 leaders recognize the abilities in
   people and work fluidly with them. They are able to mentor
   people with different talents, temperaments, and styles. While
   average leaders try to lead everyone the same way, Level 4
   leaders lead everyone differently. That takes creativity and
   confidence.

   Having said that, I must add that Level 4 leaders also bring
structure and stability to the development process. As you
develop leaders, keep in mind the following guidelines:

- *The process must occur daily.* The secret of your success is
  determined by your daily agenda. No one ever got good at
  something they seldom practiced.
- *The process must be measurable.* Although growth begins
  inwardly, it must be proven outwardly. Therefore, the goals
  of growth must be something that can be seen and verified
  by you and the person you mentor. If they don't know where
  they're going, how will they ever know if they get there?

- *The process must include things they value.* If you include things they desire, people will be motivated to achieve them.
- *The process must align with your strengths.* When people ask me to mentor them, my first question is, "In what area?" I do only a few things well and can help people only in the areas of my strengths. As you prepare to develop people, teach from those strengths and encourage those you mentor to seek out others who can help them in areas where you can't.
- *The process must fit into their dream plan.* I state in my book *Put Your Dream to the Test* that the more valid reasons a person has to achieve their dream, the higher the odds are that they will. Valid reasons also increase the odds that a person will follow through with personal growth.

> Although growth begins inwardly, it must be proven outwardly.

7. **Never Work Alone:** One of the secrets of developing leaders on Level 4 is to have the people you are mentoring beside you as often as possible so that they can learn how you think and act in a variety of situations. Your goal at first is for them to observe as you model leadership. But as quickly as you can, give them responsibilities that you can monitor. And as soon as they're ready, empower them to act on their own.

8. **Blend the Soft and Hard Sides of Development:** Level 4 leaders have to deal simultaneously with people issues and business issues, and they need to be able to do both effectively. That's an art. As you work to develop people, maintain a relational approach, valuing them and adding value to them. At the same time, do what you must to achieve a good bottom line. Write out a philosophy that will help you to do both. If it helps, write out your priorities and put them in order of importance as a guide.

9. **Take Responsibility for Energizing Others:** While it's true that the people you develop need to be self-motivated, it's also true that leaders create energy and inspire others to achieve. As you work to develop people, strive to create an emotionally engaging process that encourages those you mentor to take risks and enjoy their experiences. Too many leaders disconnect. They have a been-there-done-that mentality that is alienating, not alluring. In contrast, if you have a been-there-love-that way of thinking, people will be attracted to you and want to do their best when they engage with you.

10. **Remain Approachable As a Leader, Role Model, and Coach:** An open door and open heart invite people to come into a leader's life. That openness comes only when a leader initiates and takes responsibility for having it. I encourage you to take that responsibility, because when you do, you will develop a special connection with your people. Openness, humility, and transparency are always very attractive. These qualities give others permission to ask questions, take risks, and be themselves. And that takes leadership development to a whole new level.

Level 5:
THE PINNACLE

*The Highest Leadership Accomplishment Is
Developing Other Leaders to Level 4*

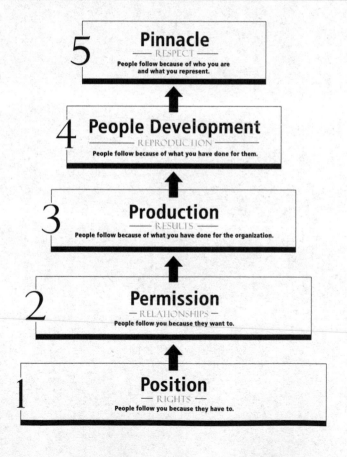

5 **Pinnacle**
— RESPECT —
**People follow because of who you are
and what you represent.**

4 **People Development**
— REPRODUCTION —
People follow because of what you have done for them.

3 **Production**
— RESULTS —
People follow because of what you have done for the organization.

2 **Permission**
— RELATIONSHIPS —
People follow you because they want to.

1 **Position**
— RIGHTS —
People follow you because they have to.

Rare is the leader who reaches Level 5—the Pinnacle. Not only is leadership at this level a culmination of leading well on the other four levels, but it also requires both a high degree of skill and some amount of natural leadership ability. It takes a lot to be able to develop other leaders so that they reach Level 4; that's what Level 5 leaders do. The individuals who reach Level 5 lead so well for so long that they create a legacy of leadership in the organization they serve.

> The individuals who reach Level 5 lead so well for so long that they create a legacy of leadership in the organization they serve.

Pinnacle leaders stand out from everyone else. They are a cut above, and they seem to bring success with them wherever they go. Leadership at this high level lifts the entire organization and creates an environment that benefits everyone in it, contributing to their success. Level 5 leaders often possess an influence that transcends the organization and the industry the leader works in.

Most leaders who reach the Pinnacle do so later in their careers. But the Pinnacle level is not a resting place for leaders to stop and view their success. It is a reproducing place from which they make the greatest impact of their lives. That's why leaders who reach the Pinnacle should make the most of it while they can. With gratitude and humility, they should lift up as many leaders as they can, tackle as many great challenges as possible, and extend their influence to make a positive difference beyond their own organization and industry.

The Upside of the Pinnacle

Your Influence Has Expanded Beyond Your Reach and Your Time

When writing about Level 1, I told you that as you climbed the 5 Levels of Leadership, the upsides would continue to increase while the downsides would decrease. However, Level 5 doesn't fit that pattern. On the Pinnacle, I see only three major upsides. But though they are few, each carries a tremendous weight and huge impact.

1. Pinnacle Leadership Creates a Level 5 Organization

Many organizations seem to struggle to maintain their existence. Others work hard to inch their way toward growth or increased profitability. Meanwhile, a few organizations rise above the rest and seem to function at an extraordinarily high level. What's their secret? Leadership. Great organizations have great leaders, and the best organizations that function at the highest capacity — Level 5 organizations — become what they are because they are led by Level 5 leaders.

General Electric has been held up as a business model for decades. Year after year it is cited by *Fortune* magazine as a top-ten organization for leadership. Why? Because for many years it was led by Jack Welch, a Level 5 leader, and his emphasis was on developing other leaders to become Level 4 leaders — leaders who produce other leaders.

Because Level 5 leaders empower many people to lead larger, they lift the leadership lid for everyone in the organization. Because they produce lots of leaders and continue to do so over the long haul of their careers, their organizations develop an abundance mind-set. People in the organization receive lots of opportunities, and they expect to continue getting them. With the development of each leader and the pursuit of every opportunity, the organization continues to get stronger. And in time, leadership becomes part of their DNA. And even when one leader steps down or retires, there are many leaders ready and able to take their place because Level 5 organizations have a pipeline of leaders being produced.

Because Level 5 leaders have worked their way up through each level to arrive at the Pinnacle position, they understand and practice leadership at a high level. They have experienced a transformation of sorts with each transition from one level to another, and as a result they have insight that helps them to recognize where other leaders are in the process and to help those leaders navigate the various changes required to move up to the next level.

2. Pinnacle Leadership Creates a Legacy within the Organization

Level 5 leaders want to do more than just run an organization well. They want to do more than succeed. They want to create a legacy. Journalist Walter Lippmann was right when he said, "The final test of a leader is that he leaves behind him in other men the convictions and the will to carry on." If you reach the Pinnacle of leadership, you have an opportunity to make an impact beyond your tenure and possibly beyond your

> "The final test of a leader is that he leaves behind him in other men the convictions and the will to carry on."
> —*Walter Lippmann*

own lifetime. You do that by developing a generation of leaders *who will develop the next generation of leaders.*

Level 5 leaders are measured by the caliber of leaders they develop, not the caliber of their own leadership. Their approach to leadership changes accordingly. Larry Bossidy, former CEO of AlliedSignal, understood this when he asked,

> How am I doing as a leader? The answer is how the people you lead are doing. Do they learn? Do they manage conflict? Do they initiate change? You won't remember when you retire what you did in the first quarter of 1994.... What you'll remember is how many people you developed.

Not only that, you'll remember how well you developed them and how effectively they were able to carry on after you were no longer leading. In Level 5 organizations, when the top leader steps down, there are usually many leaders ready to rise up and take the reins. And the organization experiences continuity unfamiliar to organizations with lesser leaders.

3. Pinnacle Leadership Provides an Extended Platform for Leading

In America, we believe everyone has the right to speak. But even in a free society, you have to earn the right to be heard. Level 5 leaders have paid their dues and earned that right. And because they lead well and develop others to do likewise, their influence extends beyond their reach. People outside of their direct sphere of influence hear about them and seek them out for advice. Level 5 leaders are able to cross lines out of their industry or area of expertise to speak with authority. People respect them for who they are and what they represent. That gives them a greater platform and extended influence. They often have a chance to make a broader impact on society or to advance the cause of leadership, redefine it, and pour themselves into the next generation of leaders.

> In America, we believe everyone has the right to speak. But even in a free society, you have to earn the right to be heard.

Think of the great leaders of government, business, education, and faith. Their influence far exceeds the organizations they led. Nelson Mandela's authority has few boundaries. Everyone respects him. Jack Welch no longer leads General Electric, but his leadership advice is sought internationally. For decades presidents of the United States have sought the counsel of Billy Graham. Their influence is extensive and their reputations are legendary.

With this extended influence comes a responsibility to steward it with integrity. Level 5 leaders understand that the highest position of leadership is not a place to be served by others but to serve others. It is not a place to receive, but a place to give.

Margaret and I recently saw evidence of such stewardship when we visited the Nobel Museum in Stockholm, Sweden. Our guide told us stories of great men and women who have made our world a better place to live. One of the Nobel recipients was Albert Einstein. He once said,

> Strange is our situation here upon earth. Each of us comes for a short visit, not knowing why, yet sometimes seeming to divine a purpose. From the standpoint of daily life, however, there is one thing we do know: that man is here for the sake of other men—above all for those upon whose smile and well-being our own happiness depends, and also for the countless unknown souls with whose fate we are connected by a bond of sympathy. Many times a day I realize how much my own outer and inner life is built upon the labors of my fellow men, both living and

dead, and how earnestly I must exert myself in order to give in return as much as I have received.

Einstein's reputation went far beyond the halls of academia and the field of physics. His influence has continued long after death. That is what happens with leaders and thinkers of his caliber. That's what happens with leaders who make it to the Pinnacle.

The leadership journey has the potential to take individuals through a lifelong process in three phases: *learn, earn, return.* People at the start of the journey who are given a position of leadership are faced with a decision. Are they going to learn now to lead better, or are they going to rely on their position, guard their turf, and play king of the hill to maintain what they've got? Those who choose to learn enter the *learning* phase and start to slowly climb up the levels of leadership. Typically, when they reach the Production level, they begin to receive recognition and the rewards of leadership. That's when most leaders enter the *earning* phase. Many are content to stay there. They climb the ladder in the organization, they have the respect of their peers, and they earn a good living. Only those leaders who decide to give back to others and develop leaders enter the *returning* phase. Leaders who dedicate themselves to developing more leaders and pour themselves into the task, giving their best energies and resources to raise up other leaders, are the only ones who have the chance to move up to the Pinnacle.

No matter where you are in your own leadership journey, I encourage you to learn all you can and keep learning. And when you reach the earning phase, don't stop there. Don't lead others solely for your own benefit. Start giving to others and teaching them to lead so that you can enter the returning phase. Do that long enough and well enough, and you give yourself an opportunity to reach Level 5 and experience its upsides.

The Downside of the Pinnacle

You May Start to Believe It's All about You

Each level of leadership has a downside. This level is no exception. But here's the good news: fewer leaders become victims of the downside at the Pinnacle level than at any other. Why? Because it's difficult to reach the Pinnacle without a great measure of maturity. Every lesson leaders learn at the previous levels becomes a curb that helps to keep them from getting off course. However, here is the bad news. Those who are susceptible to the downside on the Pinnacle fall dramatically. They can derail everything they've worked for up to this point.

Here are the three negative things you need to look out for if you reach the Pinnacle:

1. Being on the Pinnacle Can Make You Think You've Arrived

It's ironic, but one of the greatest dangers for Pinnacle leaders at the top is similar to a downside for Position leaders at the bottom: thinking they've arrived. If you came into leadership with a destination mind-set, and you carried it with you as you've moved your

> It's ironic, but one of the greatest dangers for Pinnacle leaders at the top is similar to a downside for Position leaders at the bottom: thinking they've arrived.

way up through the 5 Levels of Leadership, you may think that the Pinnacle is a place to rest, smell the roses, and make the most of your privileges. If that's your mind-set, beware!

In his book *How the Mighty Fall,* Jim Collins wrote that those who fall often have an entitlement mind-set, bolstered by arrogance. He wrote that for such leaders, "Success is viewed as 'deserved' rather than fortuitous, fleeting, or even hard earned in the face of daunting odds; people begin to believe that success will continue almost no matter what the organization decides to do, or not to do."

A leader's decisions always make an impact—for better or worse. Leaders who have reached the top of their profession or the top of their organization cannot take anything for granted. No matter how good they've been in the past, they still need to strategize, weigh decisions, plan, and execute at a high level. Momentum can overcome a lot of problems, but even great momentum cannot continually compensate for negligence, arrogance, or stupidity.

Nor should they treat the organization as their personal property— even if it *is* their property. Every organization for which people work is a trust. If you're the leader, you cannot make decisions with only you and your personal interests in mind. To whomsoever much is given, much will be required.

People who reach the top of their field are always in danger of thinking they have nothing left to learn. If that happens to you, it's the beginning of the end. To be effective, leaders must always be learners. You can never arrive—you can only strive to get better. That is the mind-set you must bring to every day of your leadership. If you're through learning, you're through.

> **If you're through learning, you're through.**

2. Being on the Pinnacle Can Lead
You to Believe Your Own Press

Few things are more ridiculous than leaders who take themselves too seriously and begin to believe they are God's gift to others. Yet it happens continually. History is filled with stories of people who got carried away with their power and position.

One such leader was King Gustavus Adolphus of Sweden. He was known as a brilliant military commander, and during his reign he elevated Sweden from a minor to a major power in Europe and ushered in what's known as the Golden Age of Sweden. But like many strong leaders, he started to believe that anything he desired to do would automatically succeed.

As the king fought in the Thirty Years War, he desired to rule the Baltic Sea. To do so, he was determined to build a ship that towered over the other ships in beauty and size. He decided on the measurements and armament of the ship, even though he had no naval expertise, and gave them to the shipbuilders. The following words were written about this venture. "Nothing can be more impressive and more dedicated to glorifying to his royal majesty than for his ship to bear the most magnificent decoration that has ever been held on the ocean."

The ship was called the *Vasa*, named after the monarch's royal house. As the war raged on, the king became impatient for its launch. Tests were made to check its stability, but the monarch would not tolerate a delay. So on August 10, 1628, *Vasa* was launched on its maiden voyage. Thousands watched as the ship slowly left the harbor in Stockholm. But as soon as the ship was exposed to a gust of wind, it began to sway. It heeled over, took on water, and sank a few hundred feet from shore less than a mile from where it began! Clearly the king's confidence wasn't enough to keep his dream afloat.

Any time a leader begins to believe his own press, he's in trouble. When people excel to a high level in their profession, a type of mythology grows up around them. They become larger than life in other people's minds. A lot of the time it's hype. No Level 5 leaders are as good as people give them credit for. And no leaders—no matter how long or how well they've led—are above the laws of leadership. The laws are like gravity. They apply to you whether or not you believe in them.

If you become a Level 5 leader, never forget that like everyone else, you started at the bottom as a positional leader. You had to work to build relationships. You had to prove your productivity. And investing in the lives of others came about only with effort. Be confident, but also be humble. If you've become successful, it's only because a lot of other people helped you all along the way.

3. Being on the Pinnacle Can Make You Lose Focus

When leaders reach Level 5, the number of opportunities they receive becomes extraordinary. Everyone wants to hear what such leaders have to say. But many of these opportunities are really little more than distractions. They won't help the leader's organization or cause.

In *Good to Great,* Jim Collins tells a story that illustrates how this can happen. The example he gives is of former Chrysler chairman Lee Iacocca. Collins writes:

> Lee Iacocca, for example, saved Chrysler from the brink of catastrophe, performing one of the most celebrated (and deservedly so) turnarounds in American business history. Chrysler rose to the height of 2.9 times the market at a point about halfway through his tenure. Then, however, he diverted his attention to making himself one of the most celebrated CEOs in American business history. *Investor's Business Daily* and the *Wall Street Journal* chronicled how Iacocca appeared regularly on talk shows like the *Today* show and *Larry King Live,* personally starred in over eighty commercials, entertained the idea of

running for president of the Unites States (quoted at one point, "Running Chrysler has been a bigger job than running the country....I could handle the national economy in six months"), and widely promoted his autobiography. The book, *Iacocca,* sold seven million copies and elevated him to rock star status.... Iacocca's personal stock soared, but in the second half of his tenure, Chrysler's stock fell 31 percent behind the general market.[1]

If leaders who reach the Pinnacle want to make the most of their time there, they must remain focused on their vision and purpose and continue leading at the highest level.

I'm sorry to admit that I've occasionally lost focus in my own leadership. It happened to me at EQUIP several years ago. During the first eight years of the company's existence, we focused on training one million leaders internationally. We called it the Million Leaders Mandate. It consumed our attention, and we put all our resources to work making it happen. When we reached our goal, we celebrated. I gave each staff member, leadership trainer, and major donor a ring in appreciation for their help. But then, we lost focus. We continued to train leaders, but we experienced a letdown. I wasn't focused on a new goal, so neither was the team. That was a big mistake, and it meant that we didn't use the momentum we had built to keep moving forward at our previous pace. The good news is that the leaders of EQUIP huddled together, identified our next big mountain, and refocused our energies once again to make the climb.

> No matter where you are in your leadership journey, never forget that what got you to where you are won't get you to the next level.

No matter where you are in your leadership journey, never forget that what got you to where you are won't get you to the next level. Each step forward requires focus and a willingness to keep learning, adapting, strategizing, and working. You don't stay on top without focus, humility, and hard work.

Best Behaviors on Level 5

How to Use the Pinnacle as a Platform to Do Something Greater Than Yourself

Leadership should always be about others, not about the leader. That's true at every level, and it's especially important on Level 5 because having people follow out of deep respect is the height of leadership. Pinnacle leaders have a lot of horsepower, and they need to make good use of it while they're on top to do more than help themselves. Here are my suggestions:

1. Make Room for Others at the Top

One of the most important things any Level 5 leader can do is make room at the top for other leaders. Most leaders make it their goal to cultivate *followers*. But gathering followers doesn't create room for other leaders. As a Pinnacle leader, you must create that room. That begins on Level 4 when you start developing leaders. If you do that continually and promote good leaders whenever you can, you create a cycle of positive change in the organization that creates room for leaders. That may seem counterintuitive. Wouldn't having more leaders create less room? No. And here's why: when you develop a leader who develops other leaders, you create more room at the top because you increase the size and power of the entire organization. Every time you develop good leaders and help find a place for them to lead and make an impact, they gather more good people to them. As a result, the organization grows (along with its potential) and it needs more good leaders. This process creates a cycle of expansion and a kind of momentum toward the top for other leaders that helps to propel the organization forward.

Developing leaders from the Pinnacle level requires great skill and intentionality. It is not easy to develop leaders. It's even more difficult to develop leaders who will devote themselves to developing other leaders instead of just leading. As I studied leaders who had only followers versus leaders who developed leaders, I began to notice some subtle but clear differences. Here are the characteristics of a Level 5 leader who develops leaders:

The Leader's Desire—Being Succeeded Instead of Needed

Early in my leadership career I loved it when people needed me. And it was music to my ears when they told me so. I loved hearing things such as "We couldn't make it without you. What would we do if you were gone? You're the only leader that really understands us." Sadly, I believed them!

The reality is that no one is indispensible. Worse, allowing others to become dependent does little more than satisfy a leader's ego. It is a very limiting leadership style that has a very short life span.

The first step in developing leaders is to have a desire to develop people so that they can succeed without you. Leadership author and former FedEx executive Fred A. Manske Jr., observed, "The ultimate leader is one who is willing to develop people to the point that they eventually surpass him or her in knowledge and ability." On the Pinnacle level, that should always be your goal.

> "The ultimate leader is one who is willing to develop people to the point that they eventually surpass him or her in knowledge and ability."
> —Fred A. Manske Jr.

The Leader's Focus — Working on People's Strengths Instead of Weaknesses

Some leaders take a counseling approach to developing people. By that I mean that they focus on what the person is doing poorly or wrong, and they focus their attention on helping them make corrections in those areas. In fact, when I began my career, I spent a lot of time counseling people. But to my great frustration, I saw little improvement in the people I worked with. To be fair, I really wasn't a good counselor. But I also had a eureka moment when I figured out the main reason we weren't making progress. I was focused on people's weaknesses. That's no way to develop people.

If you want to develop people, you must help them discover and build upon their strengths. That's where people have the most potential to grow. Helping to develop their strengths is the only way to help leaders become world-class.

The Leader's Attitude — Giving Away Power Instead of Hoarding It

Did you play follow the leader as a kid? The goal of the game was to hold onto your place in the front of the line as long as possible. The kids who won were most aggressive at trying to do something no one else could imitate. As a Level 5 leader, you need to be as aggressive about giving away power to other leaders as you were at hoarding it when you were a kid. That requires an abundance attitude, where your mind-set is "Let's Lead Together." You must become a world-class empowerer. As Lynne Joy McFarland asserted in the book *21st Century Leadership: Dialogue with 100 Top Leaders,* "The empowerment leadership model

> "The empowerment leadership model shifts away from 'position power' to 'people power' where all people are given leadership roles so they can contribute to their fullest capacity."
> —*Lynne Joy McFarland*

shifts away from 'position power' to 'people power' where all people are given leadership roles so they can contribute to their fullest capacity."

The Leader's Perspective—Seeing Potential Leaders As They Could Be Instead of As They Are

One of the keys to developing leaders—at any level—is seeing people not as they are or as others see them, but as they could be. Having a hand in closing the gap between how someone is and the fulfillment of their potential is what motivates Level 5 leaders to raise up other leaders to Level 4. Seeing *what is* takes very little talent. Seeing *what could be*—and helping to make it reality—takes vision, imagination, skill, and commitment. That's what a Pinnacle leader needs to bring to the table.

The Leader's Impact—Knowing It Takes a Level 5 Leader to Develop a Level 4 Leader

Leading and developing leaders is not easy. Leaders with high potential will only follow leaders who are ahead of them—in ability, experience, or both. Someone who is a 9 in leadership won't follow a 5. For that reason, Pinnacle leaders cannot delegate the leadership development process of potential leaders to others who are less talented than those being mentored. It simply doesn't work. If there are potential Level 4 or Level 5 leaders in your organization and you're a Level 5 leader, you must dedicate the time and effort to mentoring them. Otherwise they will go elsewhere to find a Level 5 leader who is willing to do it. The best potential leaders will not remain in the organization unless you go to them where they are, extend your hand, and help them to climb up to your level.

2. Continually Mentor Potential Level 5 Leaders

I've been teaching and writing on the subject of leadership for three and a half decades, and in that time I've had the privilege of working with a lot of organizations. Each of them has been unique with questions, needs, and conditions unlike any other. However, all of them have had one thing in common. They needed more and better leaders! Not once has anyone in an organization said, "We have too many leaders. And the ones we have are better than we want. Can you help us get rid of some?"

Recently I attended an interview between my friend Bill Hybels and former General Electric CEO Jack Welch. Bill was asking Welch questions about succession (a subject I'll address specifically in a moment). Welch said that a few years before he exited General Electric, he made a list of potential successors. The list included three categories: leaders on the inside track, leaders with potential, and long shots — and he named several people.

As he spoke, I began to wonder how he was able to choose from the inside-track leaders, but before I could go very far in my thinking, Welch amazed me by mentioning that his successor had come from the long-shot category. And that got me thinking about the importance of mentoring. I came to these conclusions:

1. You have to have a lot of good leaders to select the best leaders.
2. You must give your best to all potential Level 5 leaders because you may be surprised by who finishes the strongest.

No matter what your leadership potential may be, you should strive to work your way up to Level 4 so that you can invest in others. But if you reach Level 5, you have a much greater responsibility. No one other than a Level 5 leader can raise up other Level 5 leaders. If you make it to the Pinnacle, give your best potential leaders your best and never stop mentoring them.

3. Create an Inner Circle That Will Keep You Grounded

When leaders reach Level 4, their inner circle makes them better. The Law of the Inner Circle says that those closest to leaders determine their potential. Inner circle members help leaders take their organization to a higher level. That's still true on Level 5, but the inner circle must also fulfill another function: it must keep the leader grounded. As I've already explained, it's very easy for leaders to begin believing their own press on Level 5. A good inner circle can help leaders on the Pinnacle level to avoid that pitfall.

Jim Collins, in *How the Mighty Fall*, writes about the erosion of healthy team dynamics that can occur in highly successful organizations. "There is a marked decline in the quality and amount of dialogue and debate; there is a shift toward either consensus or dictatorial management rather than a process of argument and disagreement followed by unified commitment to execute decisions." When those things occur, the leader and the organization are headed for trouble.

On Level 5, a good inner circle will allow leaders to be themselves, but inner circle members will also tell them the truth about themselves. These things keep the journey enjoyable, prevent loneliness, and keep leaders from developing hubris. And here's the good news. The people in your inner circle can become your favorite people—like family.

4. Do Things for the Organization That Only Level 5 Leaders Can Do

Being on Level 5 allows a leader to see and do things that cannot be done from any other place in leadership. Some of those things are obvious. If you're the top leader in your organization, you need to guide it.

You need to be a good model to everyone in the organization by valuing people, continuing to grow, practicing the golden rule, being authentic, exhibiting good values, and living out the right priorities.

Other things may be less obvious and very specific to your situation and organization. You may be able to create a groundbreaking product or service. You may be able to champion a value or cause that no one else could as effectively. You may be able to help people improve their lives. You may be able to impact your community in a unique way. You may have relationships with people who can help you to do something important. All the work you've done and all the influence you've gained over the years just might be in your hands so that you can do something bigger with it. You have to keep your eyes, ears, and heart open to the possibilities. The success you have hasn't been given to you for only yourself. Level 5 leaders have a platform to lead and persuade. Whenever possible, use it to pass on those things that have helped you. Leadership is influence. Leverage it to add value to others.

5. Plan for Your Succession

In the mid-1980s, I had the privilege of spending a few days with management expert Peter Drucker. A group of leaders got a chance to sit with him, listen, take notes, and ask questions. I learned many wonderful things from Drucker, but there was one question he asked that challenged me more than anything else. During the session, he asked each one of us, "Who is going to replace you?"

Prior to that time, I had never asked myself that question. When Drucker asked it, I had no answer. But I walked away from my time with him determined to live in such a way that I would be able to answer it. And from that day forward, I dedicated myself to developing the top leaders in my sphere of influence and helping them to be ready to lead on as high a level as possible.

Leaving a successor is the last great gift a leader can give an organization. Leadership-transition difficulties are far too common, and like the passing of the baton in a relay race, a leadership transition must be planned and executed well. Success is dependent upon the leader with the baton handing it off to the next leader when both of them are running at maximum speed. Writer Lorin Woolfe says, "The ultimate test for a leader is not whether he or she makes smart decisions and takes decisive action, but whether he or she teaches others to be leaders and builds an organization that can sustain its success even when he or she is not around." True leaders put ego aside and strive to create successors who go beyond them. And they plan to hand off the baton of leadership in stride when they are still running at their peak. If a leader has already begun to slow down, the baton is being handed off too late. No leader should hurt the organization's momentum by staying too long just for his or her own gratification. The number one problem in organizations led by Level 5 leaders is that they stay too long. So if you're a Level 5 leader who runs an organization, plan your succession and leave *before* you feel you have to.

6. Leave a Positive Legacy

Someone once asked Billy Graham what the most surprising thing about life was. "The brevity of it," he replied. Now that I've entered my sixties, I would have to agree with him. When you're young, you can't wait to get somewhere in life—to achieve success, climb the ladder, make an impact. If you have a type-A personality, you move fast and try to conquer as much ground as you can. But as you age, you realize there's much more to life than success. You want to make a difference. And if you think about it early enough, you have the opportunity to leave a positive legacy. That's what I desire to do. I hope you do as well.

> Someone once asked Billy Graham what the most surprising thing about life was. "The brevity of it," he replied.

One of the keys to arriving at the end of our lives without regret is doing the work of creating a lasting legacy. If you are a Level 5 leader, I want to encourage you to use the influence you have now to create a better world. How? First, recognize that what you do daily, over time, becomes your legacy. Whether it's spending quality time with your family every day, saving money and investing every month, speaking kind and encouraging words to others each day—these actions result in a legacy of positive impact.

Second, decide now what you want your legacy to be. How do you want to be remembered? What would you like people to say about you at your funeral? Do you have a vision for the positive impact you want to leave behind you? Do you know what you can invest in potential leaders who will want to help you build it?

Finally, understand that a legacy is the sum of your whole life, not just snippets. If you have failed, that's okay. Has your life taken a path that is less than ideal? Put it behind you. Set off in the right direction and begin to change the way you live starting today. Fulfill your mission and vision for your life. Do it now before it is too late to change.

Don't let yourself get to the final days of your life wondering what could have been. Decide today what your life will be, and then take action each and every day to live your dreams and leave your legacy!

The Laws of Leadership at the Pinnacle Level

As you consider the different aspects of Level 5, please be aware of how the following laws of leadership come into play:

The Law of Respect
People Naturally Follow Leaders Stronger Than Themselves

When I wrote the overview of the 5 Levels of Leadership in the first chapter of this book, I used the word *respect* to describe Level 5. On the Pinnacle, leaders have led so well for so long that they have become

> "Every great institution is the lengthened shadow of a single man."
> —*Ralph Waldo Emerson*

larger than life, and people are influenced by their reputation even before there is any direct contact between leaders and their followers. Ralph Waldo Emerson said, "Every great institution is the lengthened shadow of a single man." That sentiment is a good description of Level 5 leaders. Their presence makes an impact.

It's true that leaders gain respect on every level. They earn it by showing worthiness for the chance to lead on Level 1, developing relationships on Level 2, creating a productive team on Level 3, and developing people on Level 4. But on Level 5 the respect they've earned begins to compound. Everyone wants to follow a true Level 5 leader.

The Law of Intuition
Leaders Evaluate Everything with a Leadership Bias

Everybody is intuitive. We all have strong intuition in the areas of our giftedness. What Level 5 leaders possess in abundance is leadership intuition, and as a result, they see everything with a leadership bias. Good leaders learn to trust what Emerson called the "blessed impulse." That's the hunch that informs you that something is right. Level 5 leaders learn to trust those instincts and act upon them.

Of all the laws of leadership that I teach, the Law of Intuition is the most difficult. Why? Because most people have a difficult time teaching in the areas where they are intuitive. Intuition is the ability to experience immediate insight without rational thought. If you can perform leadership tasks, knowing they're right but not having examined them with rational thought, it's difficult to explain why you did what you did.

The more naturally gifted you are in leadership, the stronger your leadership intuition is likely to be. Learn to trust it. And if your gifting in leadership isn't high, don't lose hope. While it's true that your leadership intuition will never be as high as that of a natural leader, you can still develop leadership intuition based on leadership experience and reflective thinking on your failures and successes.

The Law of Timing
When to Lead Is as Important as What to Do and Where to Go

Closely related to the Law of Intuition is the Law of Timing, because timing is also largely instinctive. Knowing what to do can be relatively easy for an effective leader at Level 3. Knowing the right timing can be much more difficult. Why? There are so many intangible factors. Often a hunch is all we have to rely on to make a timing decision, and that can be difficult to explain. People are apt to listen to hard facts and respect the point of view of the person who expresses them. Intuition doesn't carry as much weight—unless you have a proven track record of right assessments to back it up.

Leaders on Level 5 have so much experience and credibility that others listen to their hunches when it comes to timing. If you're not yet on Level 5, then be aware that others may not trust your advice when it comes to timing. But don't despair. Listen to your intuition, take note of when it's wrong or right, and develop a track record that will bring you the credibility you desire.

The Law of Legacy
A Leader's Lasting Value Is Measured by Succession

I've already discussed the importance of legacy on Level 5, so I don't need to say a lot here. Allow me to leave you with this thought: The goal in life is not to live forever. The goal in life is to create something that does. The best way to do that as a Level 5 leader is to invest what you have in the lives of others.

> The goal in life is not to live forever. The goal in life is to create something that does.

The Law of Explosive Growth
To Add Growth, Lead Followers—
To Multiply, Lead Leaders

Every time you develop a potential leader to Level 4, you change your organization for the better and increase its potential. Why? Because...

When you develop a follower, you gain a follower.
When you develop a leader, you gain a leader and all his followers.

When you develop a Level 4 leader, you gain a leader who creates other leaders, and you gain all the leaders and all the followers that they lead.

That is why Level 5 leaders are so powerful and why their organizations have unlimited potential!

Help Others Move Up to
Levels 4 and 5

Create Crucible Moments for the Leaders You Develop

At this point in previous sections of the book, I discussed the beliefs that would help you to move up to the next level of leadership. However, when you're on the Pinnacle level, there is no higher place in leadership. So what am I going to do in this section? Teach you how to help *others* to move up to the higher levels of leadership. Once you reach Level 5, your focus shouldn't be on advancing yourself anyway; it should be on helping *others* move up as high as they can go.

What is the secret of learning to lead? Leading. That's like saying that you learn to drive a car by driving a car. Or that you learn to cook by cooking. All are true. As novelist Mark Twain once said drily, "I know a man who grabbed a cat by the tail and learned 40 percent more about cats than the man who didn't." This may sound like a catch-22, like the old lament that you can't get a job without first having experience, yet you can't get experience without first having a job. That's where you come in.

As a mentor, you can give the inexperienced leaders leadership experiences that make them better. A little experience goes a lot further than a lot of theory. You've probably heard the saying, "When a person with money meets a person with experience, the person with experience usually gets the money and the person with the money gets the experience."

As an experienced leader, you can identify potential leaders, you can figure out what kinds of experiences they need, and you can help to provide them in a controlled environment where their failures and fumbles won't completely take them out of the game of leadership.

Can you identify the experiences that taught you invaluable leadership lessons and shaped you as a person and leader? I certainly can. These are crucible moments. While I was writing *The 21 Irrefutable Laws of Leadership*, I was surprised to discover that I could remember a specific experience for each law that cemented it in my leadership consciousness. For example, the Law of Victory had become a reality to me in 1970 when I led my organization to reach a goal that nearly everyone believed was impossible. The Law of the Inner Circle became clear to me on my fortieth birthday when I had to admit to myself that I was not as successful as I had hoped to be, and if I was going to accomplish all that I desired to, I needed to develop an inner circle of other leaders to work alongside me.

The key incidents in your life—crucible moments—have shaped you. They've created breakthroughs for you. And the leadership experiences you've had—both good and bad—have made you the leader you are today. The same will be true for those you lead and develop. Why not help others experience as many positive breakthroughs as possible while they are under your care?

I recently read an article by Robert J. Thomas in the *MIT Sloan Management Review* that confirms my observations on leadership development. Thomas argues that organizations that do a good job developing leaders use crucible experiences as "a kind of superconcentrated form of leadership development." He writes,

Crucibles can occur on and off the job. Some take the form of reversal—a death in the family, a divorce, the loss of a job. Others involve a suspension, an in-between period that people go through while in graduate school, boot camp, unemployment—

even jail. A third form is the crucible of new territory, in which the individual is thrust into a new social role or asked to take on an overseas assignment in an unfamiliar country.[2]

Thomas goes on to describe two very dissimilar organizations that orchestrate and manage crucible experiences to help their leaders develop and grow: the Mormon Church and the Hells Angels. Thomas asserts,

> Both organizations are large, durable, complex, multiunit, multinational entities that have grown rapidly in the past three decades. Both have closed borders and engage in selective recruitment of new members, and they rarely admit converts into the top leadership ranks. Yet neither suffers from a weak leadership gene pool. Each group uses a particular activity as a crucible experience for leader development.
>
> For the Mormon Church, the most visible crucible is the missionary experience, a test of faith, identity and leadership talent that also serves as the principal growth engine for church membership. For the Hells Angels, it takes the form of the motorcycle "run"—an event remarkable in its functional similarity to that of a missionary tour of duty. A brief analysis of these organizationally instigated crucibles shows how they contribute to experience-based leader development.[3]

Thomas also points out, less dramatically, that Toyota, Boeing, General Electric, and MIT also take an experiential approach to leadership development.

If you want to make the most of your influence on Level 5, then you need to create crucible moments that will enable your best leaders to reach their leadership potential. Here's how I suggest you go about doing it.

1. Identify and Create the Crucial Leadership Lessons They Must Learn

Begin by identifying the essential qualities and skills any good leader must possess. This will be your blueprint for introducing key experiences and testing potential leaders as they become ready. Here is a list I developed after my fortieth birthday when I realized I needed to dedicate myself to developing my inner circle of leaders:

Integrity	Problem-Solving
Vision	Communication
Influence	Creativity
Passion	Teamwork
Servanthood	Attitude
Confidence	Self-Discipline

Once I had settled on the list, I began to look for opportunities to put leaders in situations where they could learn experience-based lessons in those areas. For example, whenever there was a problem in the organization, I didn't solve it myself. Instead, I sent one of the leaders I was developing to try to figure it out. Afterward, we'd discuss how he or she solved the problem and what he or she learned. To help their communication, when leaders were ready, I'd give them an opportunity to speak: to various groups, to the leaders, or to the entire organization. Afterward we'd talk about what went wrong and what went right, and what they could do the next time to improve. If I wanted to help them develop their influence and improve their teamwork, I'd ask them to recruit a team of volunteers for an event or a program and work with that team to follow through. You get the idea. When you lead an organization, you can't be focused on just fulfilling the vision or getting work done. Every challenge, problem, opportunity, or initiative is a chance for you to pair potential leaders to a leadership development experience that will change who they are. Try to think in those terms every day.

2. Look for Unexpected Crucible Moments They Can Learn From

People don't learn things just because we want them to. Level 5 leaders understand that teachable moments often come as the result of "levers" in their lives. Change occurs in people's lives when they ...

Hurt enough that they have to (Pain and Adversity),
Learn enough that they want to (Education and Experience), or
Receive enough that they are able to (Support and Equipping).

Wise leaders look for moments that fall into those three categories. Some can be created, but many simply occur. Good leaders help the people they are mentoring to learn from them and make the most of them by explaining the experience and asking the right questions.

For example, when people describe a loss in their life, I do more than just sympathize with them. I ask them to tell me what they've learned from it. That's the only way in life to turn a loss into a gain. The greater the loss, the greater the potential lesson and crucible opportunity for leadership development. All of us experience far more than we understand. Your job as a Level 5 leader is to help the high-level people you are developing to make sense out of what they experience and find value in it.

3. Use Your Own Crucible Moments As Guidelines to Teach Others

Every leader needs to draw upon his or her own crucible experiences and breakthroughs as material to help the next generation of leaders

lead. To do that, you must have examined those experiences and identified the lessons you've learned from
them. It's very likely that the experiences and lessons that allowed you to
break through the leadership lids in
your life will help others break through
theirs.

> The experiences and lessons that allowed you to break through the leadership lids in your life will help others break through theirs.

My recommendation is that you set
aside time with pen and paper (or computer) to identify your own crucible moments. Then figure out how they might be able to help the
people you're developing. Here are the categories I used to analyze my
leadership crucible experiences:

Ground Breakers

These are experiences that encourage people to start developing a
leadership quality or discipline. For example, in 1972 when someone
challenged me to articulate a concrete personal development plan that
I was using to grow — and I couldn't — I made a commitment to adopt
a personal growth plan and follow it daily.

Ice Breakers

These experiences help leaders to move forward after a period of
stagnation. For example, in 1980 I made the difficult decision to leave
the organization I had been with for my entire career to work in a different one that I believed would afford me more opportunities to reach
my potential.

Cloud Breakers

These experiences lift leaders higher, allowing them to see things
as they could be. As a pastor of a small church, I began to visit large
churches and interview their leaders. This gave me insight into a much
larger world outside of my own limited experience.

Tie Breakers

These experiences allow people to make a decision that will determine their leadership direction. In 1995 I left an organization that I had led successfully so that I could start and lead a company of my own that had unlimited potential.

Heart Breakers

These experience cause leaders to stop and evaluate where they are and what they are doing. I had a heart attack in 1998. It changed my entire perspective on life, family, work, and leadership. I turned my attention to my health, and I planned how I would purposely live my days.

Record Breakers

These experiences are exhilarating, as they allow leaders to break through their leadership lids. When EQUIP reached its million-leader goal—which had seemed nearly impossible when we set it—I realized that the team and I were capable of more than we imagined if we worked together.

The purpose of reflecting on and listing your leadership breakthroughs is to share them with other potential leaders. Why do coaches have past successful players come back to the team and tell stories of past victories? Why do companies elevate past leaders who built the organization, making them legends that live beyond their years of service? Why does the Church remember heroes of the faith? Why do we study great leaders from history? For that matter, why do I share so many of my own stories? Leaders do these things because they hope that the stories will inspire another generation of leaders to reach its potential.

I want to encourage you to identify your breakthrough experiences and tell them as stories to the leaders you desire to develop. At the same time, I have to warn you: some people will call you arrogant or egocentric when you tell them. Don't let that deter you. I know of no better way to communicate important truths to others. People have been using stories to teach life's lessons for as long as human beings have been walking the earth. Tell yours and help the next generation to take its place as leaders.

4. Expose Them to Other People and Organizations That Will Impact Them

One of the best ways I found to instill leadership qualities and skills into my developing leaders was to ask them to interview good leaders. Asking questions and looking for ways to develop a certain quality is a wonderful way for a person to grow. First, they have to keep their eyes open for good leaders and well-led organizations, which begins to develop a leadership awareness in them. Second, they have to take the initiative (and sometimes be persuasive) to get the interview. Third, they have to prepare for the interview, which causes them to go deeper in their thinking about leadership. Fourth, the experience of the interview itself puts them in another leader's world and exposes them to another culture that helps them to grow. And finally, analyzing the interview and talking about it with the person who gave them the assignment helps to make the lessons concrete—especially if they are required to implement and teach what they've learned. Many a time after I asked my developing leaders to do an interview, they came back and said, "I thought that this leadership quality was strong in my life until I witnessed it in their life. I've got a long way to go."

I learned the value of experiences with great leaders and well-led organizations from my father, Melvin Maxwell. Dad introduced me to Norman Vincent Peale when I was in the seventh grade. Dr. Peale was an excellent communicator with a positive attitude. He made a strong impression on me to maintain a positive attitude. Dad also introduced me to E. Stanley Jones when I was in high school. This giant of the Christian faith was a missionary, a writer, and the founder of a renewal movement. These and other experiences at the initiative of my father marked my life as a very young person.

I've tried to emulate my father in a similar way both with my family and the leaders in my organizations. For example, when my son Joel was sixteen, Margaret and I arranged for him to meet Mother Teresa in India. Joel's most prized possession is a picture of the two of them together. And during the 1990s when my church needed to expand its vision to be challenged to grow, I took one hundred of the leaders to South Korea to visit what was then the largest church in the world. It changed their entire perspective.

Leaders on Level 5 have access to leadership, organizations, opportunities, and experiences that your emerging leaders don't. Make the most of them for their benefit. Even if you are not yet on the Pinnacle level, you still have access that your leaders don't. Share it. You can give your leaders experiences that will impact them for the rest of their lives and that may continue to create leadership ripples in future generations. Don't squander that opportunity.

As a Pinnacle level leader, you never know how great the impact will be each time you develop a Level 4 leader. Consider this. In ancient Greece, there was a leader named Socrates. No doubt you've heard of him. You may be surprised to know that even though he was an important philosopher, one who is still influential today, Socrates never wrote anything. However, one of the people he mentored did. That leader's name was Plato. Unlike his mentor, Plato founded his own academy, where he taught and mentored other leaders and thinkers. One of those young leaders was a man named Aristotle, perhaps the most influential today of all the thinkers and philosophers of ancient Greece.

When Aristotle was a young man, he was approached by Philip of Macedonia, who was looking for a tutor for his son, who was thirteen. That boy was Alexander, who became one of the greatest generals and rulers in the history of the Western world. We know him today as Alexander the Great. Experts disagree about how long Aristotle mentored young Alexander, some saying as little as a year and others as long as eight. But it seems clear that the student of Plato had a profound impact on his young charge.

It's said that Alexander once asked Aristotle, "How many is one?" The question was very simple, yet the boy was no fool, so Aristotle wondered how he should respond. Should his answer be philosophical? Mathematical? Theological? Dramaturgical?

"I'll give you an answer tomorrow," the teacher replied.

The next day, Aristotle gave him an answer: "One can be a great many." In other words, one can make a huge impact—especially when that one is a leader! And in Alexander's case, one did make a great impact. Before age thirty, Alexander had conquered the Western world.

Every time you develop a leader, you make a difference in the world. And if you develop leaders who take what they've learned and use it to develop other leaders, there's no telling what kind of an impact you'll have or how long that impact will last.

Guide to Being Your Best at Level 5

As you reflect on the upsides, downsides, best behaviors, and beliefs related to the Pinnacle level of leadership, use the following guidelines to help you grow as a leader and develop others to become Level 4 leaders.

1. **Remain Humble and Teachable:** The greatest potential internal danger of working your way up to Level 5 is thinking you've arrived and you have all the answers. That can lead to an arrogance that has the potential to derail you and your organization. The best way to guard against that is to remain teachable. To help you develop and maintain that attitude, do three things:

   - Write a credo for learning that you will follow every day; it should describe the attitude and actions you will embrace to remain teachable.
   - Find one or more people who are ahead of you in leadership that you can meet with periodically to learn from.
   - Dedicate yourself to a hobby, task, or physical activity that you deem worth your time but will also challenge you greatly and humble you.

   These three activities should help you to remember that you haven't arrived and that you still have much to learn.

2. **Maintain Your Core Focus:** If you've made it to the Pinnacle level of leadership, you possess a primary skill set—a sweet spot or strength zone—that got you there. Don't allow yourself to be distracted from using it. Identify that core strength and write out a plan for making the most of it in the coming years.

3. **Create the Right Inner Circle to Keep You Grounded:** All successful leaders need an inner circle of people who will work alongside them to achieve the vision, help them to enjoy the journey, and keep them grounded. Who are the people who will fulfill these roles in your life? Identify them and invite them into your life and leadership. My inner circle has become one of my greatest joys in life. Here is what I ask them to do:

- Love me unconditionally.
- Represent me according to my values.
- Watch my back.
- Complement my weaknesses.
- Continue to grow.
- Fulfill their responsibilities with excellence.
- Be honest with me.
- Tell me what I need to hear, not what I want to hear.
- Help carry the weight, not be an extra weight.
- Work together as a team.
- Add value to me.
- Enjoy the journey with me.

The people in my inner circle give me these things, and in return I give them my loyalty, love, and protection; I reward them financially; I develop them in leadership; I give them opportunities; and I share my blessings.

4. **Do What Only You Can Do:** There are always a handful of things that only the top leaders can do for their organization, department, or team. What are yours? Have you dedicated

time to thinking that through? If not, do it now. And make sure you make them a high priority.

5. **Create a Supercharged Leadership Development Environment:** One of the most important factors in creating a Level 5 organization is developing and maintaining an environment where leaders are constantly being developed. If you lead an organization, you must take responsibility for creating it. Strategize ways to create that environment and to promote leadership development at every level of the organization. And be sure to release your best leaders to spend time developing others. It must not be an extra; it must be part of their core responsibilities.

6. **Create Room at the Top:** Take a look at your organizational chart. Are there openings available for talented leaders who desire to move up? Take a look at the leaders who are near the top of the chart. Of what caliber are they? How long have they been with the organization? How long are they likely to stay? Are they so firmly entrenched that the talented leaders below them in the organization have little hope of advancing? If there are no openings and the leaders you have aren't going anywhere, then there is no room at the top for other potential leaders. How can you create some? What new challenges can you give your existing top leaders to open up their current positions to others? What kinds of expansion or types of initiatives could your organization tackle that would require additional leaders? If you don't create room at the top for developing leaders, you will waste much of your potential horsepower, and you will eventually start to lose your up-and-coming talent.

7. **Develop Your Top Leaders:** Level 5 leaders need to dedicate themselves to developing the top leaders in their organization. Anyone who has the potential to lead as well as you do (or even

better) should be on your radar for one-on-one mentoring. Begin with the best of the best. If you're not setting aside time every week to work with these leaders, begin doing so today. And make sure you use the crucible moments to develop them by doing the following:

- Identify the lessons all good leaders need to learn.
- Find ways to teach each of those lessons.
- Teach from your own crucible moments.
- Expose them to people who will positively impact them.
- Capitalize on unexpected crucible moments.

8. **Plan Your Succession:** As I already mentioned, Peter Drucker is the person who got me to thinking about succession in my organization. Prior to his asking about it, I honestly hadn't given it much thought. What about you? Have you thought about who would be able to step into your leadership position if you were no longer in it? If you have developed a lot of Level 4 leaders, then begin focusing on the few who have the best potential to succeed you. If you haven't been developing high-caliber leaders, then start there. Begin to help your Level 3 leaders move up to Level 4.

9. **Plan Your Legacy:** It's been said that Alfred Nobel read his own obituary, which had been mistakenly published in the newspaper, and that prompted him to change his focus from manufacturing explosives to rewarding scientists and states-men who advanced the cause of peace and development. He recognized that he wanted to create a positive legacy during his time on earth. What legacy do you want to leave? What will the end result be of your leadership efforts and career? Don't wait for someone else to determine what your life stood for. Identify it while you're still able to affect it, and start doing whatever you must to try to fulfill your legacy.

10. **Use Your Leadership Success as a Platform for Something Greater:** If you are a Pinnacle leader, then people respect you outside of your organization and industry, and you have a reputation that gives you a high degree of credibility. How will you use it? What opportunities do you have to contribute to causes greater than your own? Give that some thought, and then leverage your ability for the benefit of others outside of your direct sphere of influence.

Portrait of a Level 5 Leader

Coach John Wooden

My favorite birthday of all time was February 20, 2003. That was the day I got to meet and have lunch with one of my heroes — not a general or politician or movie star. I got time with a teacher named John Wooden, who happened to be the most successful and well-known college basketball coach in the world. He taught young men at UCLA to play basketball and — more important — how to live a successful life. He was a Level 5 leader through and through.

My admiration and respect for John Wooden began when I was just a kid. You see, basketball was my first love. I'll never forget the day in fourth grade when I attended a high school varsity basketball game. It enthralled me. For the next dozen years, I played basketball just about every day. And because I was a great fan of the game, I knew about Wooden. How could I not! During his tenure with the UCLA Bruins, Wooden won 620 games in twenty-seven seasons. His teams won ten NCAA titles during his last twelve seasons, including seven in a row from 1967 to 1973. At one point, his teams had a record winning streak of 88 consecutive games. They had four perfect 30-0 seasons.[1] They also won 38 straight games in NCAA tournaments and a record 98 straight home-game wins at Pauley Pavilion. John Wooden was named NCAA College Basketball's Coach of the Year in 1964, 1967, 1969, 1970, 1971, 1972, and 1973. In 1967 he was named the Henry Iba Award USBWA College Basketball Coach of the Year. In

1972, he received *Sports Illustrated* magazine's Sportsman of the Year award. He was named to the Basketball Hall of Fame as a coach in 1973, becoming the first to be honored as both a player and a coach.[2] When I got the chance to actually meet him in person, I was beside myself. I'd admired the man for almost forty years! How often do you get the chance to meet one of your greatest heroes? And for it to happen on my birthday simply made it sweeter.

A Day with Coach

My day with Coach Wooden started at his favorite restaurant. For the first thirty minutes over lunch, we chatted and got acquainted. Coach was a delight and very easy to talk to. Before long, I opened up a notebook I had brought with me and requested, "Mr. Wooden, would you mind if I asked you some questions?" I had spent several hours preparing for my meeting, since there were many things I wanted to learn from him. After graciously agreeing to answer my questions, he patiently did so for the next three hours, starting at the restaurant and finishing at his home nearby.

John Wooden was more than a teacher and coach. He was a homespun philosopher. His thoughts and theories have been recorded in dozens of books. But reading about him and knowing his quotes couldn't hold a candle to hearing from the man himself. Coach exuded an inner dignity that made me feel worthy and humble at the same time. The wisdom of his words was amplified by the extraordinary character he displayed in his life. I didn't just meet the coach; I experienced him.

As Coach spoke, I carefully wrote notes, and his ideas had extra credibility to me because I could feel his concern for me and desire to be helpful. Integrity, respect, and kindness pervaded everything he said. His wisdom was the result of his having lived by his principles for ninety-three years. Even more striking, everything he did seemed effortless.

During our conversation, Coach showed me a card that was important to him. He said that his father had given it to him when he was twelve. (That would have been in 1922!) Coach said that he read it every day, and he always did his best to live what it said. On the card was written:

Making the Most of One's Self

Be true to yourself.
Make each day your masterpiece.
Help others.
Drink deeply from good books.
Make friendship a fine art.
Build shelter against a rainy day.
Pray for guidance and give thanks for your blessings every day.

I believe the people who knew him would agree that he succeeded in following his father's advice, and his efforts made an extraordinary impact on the lives of many people. That day, as I left John Wooden, I realized that I had been in the presence of an extraordinary man—a true Level 5 leader.

I was fortunate to get the chance to meet John Wooden. I was even more fortunate that for the next seven years I had the privilege of meeting with him several more times and continuing to learn from him—for while he had made a great impression on me from afar, he made an even stronger one up close. In fact, when I teach the 5 Levels of Leadership and I am asked to give an example of a Level 5 leader, John Wooden is the person I most often talk about, because I think that by studying his life anyone can learn great leadership lessons. And as the closing thought in this book, I'd like to show you how John Wooden's life exemplified the 5 Levels of Leadership.

Level 1 Position—People Follow You Because
They Have To

John Wooden coached basketball for thirty years. Like all leaders, he started by receiving a leadership position and got the opportunity to make the most of it. Many coaches rely very heavily on their positions. Their attitude is *I'm the coach; you're the player. Do it my way.* That's not always the best approach to take, but there are moments when it's appropriate. And Coach used his position when needed, though he did it with a soft touch.

For example, Coach Wooden's practices were not long, but he demanded the full attention of every player each time they practiced. If a player lost focus and slacked off, Coach would kick him out of practice.

Coach Wooden told me once that the bench was the greatest power a coach had in getting the best out of his players. If they failed to play the game his way, he would use his position as coach to put them on the bench and not allow them to play in the game. That happened to Sidney Wicks, a very gifted basketball player at UCLA. The first day that Sidney joined the team and practiced with them, everyone knew that he was the most talented player on the team. However, he also came to the program with a very selfish attitude. He wanted to play the game his way and not do what Coach Wooden required.

Coach said that Sidney spent a lot of time sitting on the bench his first year on the team. That frustrated Sidney, because he wasn't playing as much as he wanted to. Coach told me Sidney would say, "Why can't I play more? You know I'm the best player on the team!" Coach would reply, "Yes Sidney, you're the best player on the team, but the team doesn't play their best when you're in the game."

Being the coach of the team gave Wooden authority, and with someone like Sidney, he had to use his authority—at least in the beginning. When needed, Coach didn't hesitate to use his position. But like all great leaders, he realized the limitations of positional leadership and did all he could to increase his influence with his players. Position may get a leader compliance from players, but it won't give championships. For his team to do better, Coach knew he had to function at a higher level of leadership, which he did.

> Position may get a leader compliance from players, but it won't give championships.

Level 2 Permission—People Follow You Because They Want To

One of John Wooden's heroes was Mother Teresa. He often quoted her, saying, "A life not lived for others is not a life." Coach also lived those words. He built strong relationships with his players, and he always did what was right for them. For example, Wooden's first college coaching job was at Indiana State in 1947, after his World War II service in the U.S. Navy. That first year, his basketball team won the Indiana Collegiate Conference title. As a result, they received an invitation to the National Association of Intercollegiate Basketball (NAIB) National Tournament in Kansas City. But Wooden declined the invitation. Why? At that time, the NAIB had a policy that banned African-Americans from playing in the tournament, and Coach was not willing to exclude Clarence Walker, one of his players who was black, from playing. However, the next year when Coach again led Indiana State to the conference title, he accepted the invitation for the same tournament after learning that the organization had reversed its policy banning African-American players. Wooden coached his team to the tournament final, where his players lost to Louisville. (That was the only championship game his teams ever lost during Coach's career.) And Clarence Walker became the first African-American player in postseason tournament play.[3]

Throughout his long career, Coach's relationships with all of his players were special. And after his career as a coach was completed, he maintained his close ties to the men he had once led on the court. Every time I visited him, our conversation was interrupted by a phone call from one of his former players checking to see how he was doing.

> "If, as a leader, you listen to them, then they'll listen to you."
> —*John Wooden*

And every time we rode in a car together, he would ask to stop at the post office so that he could mail letters he'd written in response to people who wrote to him or asked him to autograph something. More than once he told me, "If, as a leader, you listen to them, then they'll listen to you." He understood that leaders listen, learn, and then they lead.

After he died, I had the privilege of attending Coach John Wooden's memorial service at UCLA's Pauley Pavilion on June 26, 2010. His pastor, Dudley Rutherford, said,

During the last week of his life, I told Coach, "Do you remember all those autographs you signed?" And he said, "Yes." (It was at this moment where we didn't know how much longer he was going to be with us.) I said, "Coach, all those people are praying for you right now. All that love you gave, that kindness you showed, those people are all praying for you this very moment." And he smiled. Coach would be humbled today by all the attention he's receiving, but we really didn't have a choice, now did we? Because we were compelled to gather here today to celebrate his life. I was thinking about how Coach would always generously greet and sign his signature…all the autographs that he gave. And I'm wondering today, just show of hands: How many of you have in your possession, at your house, your home, you have something he signed to you? Raise your hand if you have something Coach signed.

I looked around the arena as thousands of hands were lifted. I would estimate that 80 percent of the people in attendance raised their hands. It was a reflection of Coach's kindness and his willingness to make others feel special.

Coach sure made me feel special. I was especially honored when he asked me to write a foreword for his book *A Game Plan for Life*. What a privilege! It was my chance to do something for someone who had done so much for me. Likewise, I was delighted when Coach offered to write a foreword for my next book, *Sometimes You Win, Sometimes You Learn*. With the assistance of Don Yeager, his co-writer, it was one of the last things Coach wrote before his death.

Coach Wooden had such a great personal touch. Each time I visited him, after we said our good-byes, I would take the elevator down from his condo and walk outside to the visitor's parking area. As I reached my car I would turn around and look up toward the balcony of his unit. And there would be Coach, watching me leave and waving good-bye to me. That will always be my fondest memory of him—warmly connecting as any good Level 2 leader would.

Level 3 Production—People Follow You Because of What You Have Done for the Organization

Leaders on Level 3 produce, and that can certainly be said of John Wooden. As both a player and a coach, he was a winner. He learned to shoot baskets on a hoop his father had forged himself. He took his high school basketball team to the Indiana state championship three years, winning it once. He was a three-time All-American at Purdue, leading his team to two Big Ten titles and a national championship. And he was inducted into the Naismith Memorial Hall of Fame as a player long before his induction as a coach.

Coach was a great athlete who could play many sports. He won basketball championships as a player, but his single greatest athletic feat might have occurred on a golf course. *Golf Digest* lists John Wooden as one of only four people to hit both a double eagle and a hole in one in the same round of golf. That feat was accomplished in 1947 at the South Bend Country Club in South Bend, Indiana.

Wooden started his career as a high school coach and an English teacher. His first year coaching basketball, his team had a losing record. That's significant because it was the only time *in his entire coaching career* that he had a losing record! In his eleven years coaching high school players, his record was 218-42.[4]

After coaching the 1947–48 high school season, Wooden became the head coach at UCLA. He had originally pursued the head coaching position at the University of Minnesota, since he and his wife, Nell, wanted to remain in the Midwest. And the Golden Gophers actually offered him the position, but he didn't hear about it until he had accepted the job at UCLA. And since he had given the California university his word, he declined Minnesota's offer.

Coach Wooden turned around UCLA's basketball program in one season. Prior to his arrival, they had experienced a losing season. His first year as UCLA's coach, the team won the Pacific Coast Conference (PCC) Southern Division Championship with a 22-7 record. It was the most wins in a season for UCLA since their basketball program had begun in 1919.[5] The rest of Wooden's professional career has become legendary. A career record of 885-203 (.813 winning percentage). Ten national championships. Four undefeated seasons. Named NCAA Coach of the Year seven times.[6] And in 2009, he was named by the *Sporting News* as the greatest coach of all time in any sport.[7]

Since he had experienced such a productive career as a leader, I wondered what he missed most about coaching. So I asked him. His answer surprised me: "What I miss the most are the practices, not the games." He explained, "I wanted to win every single game I ever played in or coached. But, I understood that ultimately the winning or losing may not be under my control. What was under my control was how I prepared myself and our team. I judged my success, my 'winning,' on that. It just made more sense." Coach summed up: "Winning games, titles, and championships isn't all it's cracked up to be, but getting there, the journey, is a lot more than it's cracked up to be." That's great perspective from a great leader who always produced on Level 3.

Level 4 People Development—People Follow You Because of What You Have Done for Them

Coach Wooden said, "Success is peace of mind which is a direct result of self-satisfaction in knowing you did your best to become the best that you are capable of becoming." That's what Level 4 leaders want for themselves and those they lead: to reach their potential.

> "Success is peace of mind which is a direct result of self-satisfaction in knowing you did your best to become the best that you are capable of becoming."
> —John Wooden

As well as any leader I've ever studied, Coach selected the most talented people he could find and then developed them to become the best they could be. The list of players on his UCLA teams is a Who's Who of great players: Kareem Abdul-Jabbar, Bill Walton, Sidney Wicks, Walt Hazzard, Gail Goodrich, Keith Wilkes, Curtis Rowe, Marques Johnson, Dave Meyers, and Lucius Allen. Yet Coach was more proud of his players' accomplishments in life than their achievements on a basketball court. His face would light up as he talked about the men who fulfilled leadership responsibilities in education, government, religion, and business. These were the people he developed. Time and again, his players said that Coach's desire was to use basketball to teach them how to live and lead, not to win championships.

How did Coach Wooden succeed so effectively on Level 4? Here is my take on it.

He Was Successful in Analyzing and Selecting Players

Coach always picked players who would not only play basketball well but also be good team members, good students, and good citizens. He did that by analyzing four areas:

- **Transcripts:** Coach wanted good students on his team. He believed their primary goal in entering college was to receive a good education, not to play basketball. He searched for and found true student-athletes.
- **Family Life:** Coach often said that a person's priorities should be family, faith, and friends. And regarding putting family ahead of faith, he would say with a twinkle in his eye, "God understands." By that I think he meant that you learn a lot about people's characters from how they treat their families. For example, he told me about a recruiting trip where he and an assistant visited the top high school prospect in the country. Coach had the scholarship papers with him to give to the young man if the visit went well. It didn't. During their time together, the boy spoke disrespectfully several times to his mom. Coach left without offering the scholarship. Afterward, the assistant expressed his surprise. Coach replied, "Any player that doesn't respect his mother won't respect his coach."
- **Composite Evaluation from Coaches:** Coach used to say, "If you can see a player only once, it's better to have never seen him." To get a clear perspective of players he was interested in, he would ask five coaches who opposed that player's team, "Who was the best player you coached against this year?" And then he would also talk to the head coach of that player. Only after all that would he consider evaluating him for a scholarship offer.

- **Quickness:** Leaders always need to consider what single characteristic is most important (after character) for the people on their team. Basketball is a game of quickness, so Coach chose that athletic skill over any other. That is how he was able to win his first national championship with a team where every starter was six foot five or shorter. His goal was to have the quickest players on the court so that they would have the turnover advantage. He reasoned that if his team could cause five or more turnovers than their opponent during a game, it would give them five additional attempts to score, leading to a five- or six-point advantage. That would often mean the difference between winning and losing a game.

Like all good leaders, Coach Wooden had a clear picture of who he wanted on his team. As a result, he recruited the best players — people who would have potential to be developed and win championships.

His Teaching Was Conducive to Player Development

As I've already stated, you can't win without good players. But if you have good players, you still may not win. To have a chance, you must develop them. At that, John Wooden was world-class. And his method was so simple, anyone can follow it:

1. **Explanation** — *Tell them* what you want them to know and do.
2. **Demonstration** — *Show them* what you want them to know and do.
3. **Initiation** — Let them *show you* that they know what to do.
4. **Correction** — Ask them to *change* what they are doing incorrectly.
5. **Repetition** — Ask them to do it right *over and over* again.

After that, Coach would let the results speak for themselves. He used to say, "If you prepare properly, you may be outscored, but you will never lose. You always win when you make the full effort to do the best of which you're capable."

> "You always win when you make the full effort to do the best of which you're capable."
> —John Wooden

He Developed Values and Qualities in Players to Help Them Experience True Success

I first became aware of Coach Wooden's Pyramid of Success in the 1970s when I was a young aspiring leader. He began developing it in the mid-1930s and finalized it in 1948.[8] That was when he began teaching it to his players. It gave him a concrete way of teaching them what he considered important. He taught it to others until he died.

When I discovered the pyramid in a magazine, I cut it out and taped it onto my filing cabinet so that I could review it every day. I realized that within the pyramid were qualities and values that I needed to embrace and possess. I pass it on to you. (See pyramid on the next page.)

Coach Wooden considered the values he taught to be much more important than basketball.

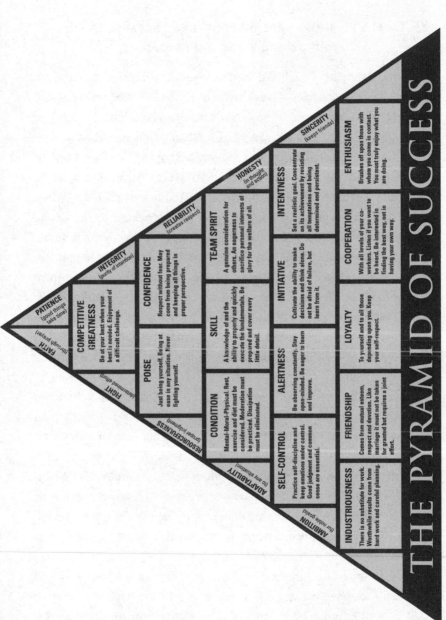

THE PYRAMID OF SUCCESS

Level 5 Pinnacle — People Follow You Because of Who You Are and What You Represent

I have no doubt that Coach Wooden reached the Pinnacle level of leadership. There is evidence of it everywhere. Since 1977, the most coveted player of the year award in basketball has been the John R. Wooden Award. It is basketball's equivalent of football's Heisman Trophy, with the winner announced during a ceremony held at the Los Angeles Athletic Club. Two annual men's basketball events called the John R. Wooden Classic and the John R. Wooden Tradition are held in Wooden's honor. And on July 23, 2003, John Wooden went to the White House where the president of the United States presented him with the Presidential Medal of Freedom, the nation's highest civilian honor.

Further evidence of the respect Coach Wooden has received from others could be seen at his memorial service at UCLA's Pauley Pavilion. Thousands of people attended, including many of his former players. Wooden was most proud of their accomplishments after they left basketball, and their individual successes are a testament to his ability to develop leaders.

During the ceremony, spotlights emphasized Coach's life and accomplishments. A light shone on his seat in the arena where he had watched the Bruins play after he had retired. That seat has now been retired, and no one else will ever sit there again. A light shone on the basketball court so that everyone would notice the names of Nell and John Wooden, for whom the court was named. Lights were shone on the ten National Championship banners to remind everyone of his coaching accomplishments, which will never be repeated in men's college basketball.

Yet, in spite of all the accomplishments and awards, the depth of Wooden's leadership can be best measured by his character. Pastor Dudley Rutherford echoed this at Coach's memorial service when he said,

I told his family at his private funeral that his greatness lies not in what he did; his greatness lies not in what he taught. His greatness lies in who he was; his character, his values, his convictions, his faith. And although he battled some health issues during the last couple of years of his life, he never once contracted the malignancy of pride. No physician ever diagnosed him as having the syndrome of selfishness. EKG revealed no trace of ego, and no MRI ever showed the slightest taint of prejudice. Morally, he had a clean bill of health. Spiritually, he was a humble man who had put his faith and trust and belief in God and in God's one and only Son, the Lord Jesus Christ. And although Coach was never boisterous about his faith—he was never obnoxious about his faith; he never pushed it on anybody—he simply lived day by day trusting, walking, living, believing in the one who was the Savior and his Lord.

During the service, broadcaster Dick Enberg described his last visit with John Wooden. As Enberg stood up to leave, Coach had smiled and pointed to his forehead. Enberg described how he walked over and kissed Coach's forehead, saying, "It was like kissing God." Coach loved a quote attributed to Socrates: "I pray thee, O God, that I may be beautiful within." That was John Wooden's prayer, and I believe God answered it.

At the close of the memorial service the people who attended did not exit quickly. They had spent two hours honoring a wonderful leader, and afterward they just wanted to stay and soak up the atmosphere. I believe many were thinking, *I want to live and die like he did.* I know I was.

Many times people don't find out how wonderful a leader was until he dies. They go to the funeral or memorial service, and they are surprised to discover how many other lives were impacted by the person. In the case of Coach, we didn't have to wait to find that out. Players from four decades of teams had received the benefit of his leadership, and so did the people they have led after their days on the court. And millions more had watched from afar as he led teams to victory. I wish I were more like him: giver, grower, teacher, coach, leader, and friend. He was wise, honest, principled, disciplined, humble, humorous, courageous, and faithful. He was a Level 5 leader. The world needs more like him.

Notes

You Can Have a Leadership Game Plan for Your Life

1. John C. Maxwell, *The 21 Irrefutable Laws of Leadership: Revised and Updated 10th Anniversary Edition* (Nashville: Thomas Nelson, 2007).

Level 1: Position

1. D. Michael Abrashoff, *It's Your Ship* (New York: Warner Books, 2002), 4.
2. "Trouble Finding the Perfect Gift for Your Boss—How About a Little Respect?" Ajilon Office, 14 October 2003, http://www.ajilonoffice.com/articles/af_bossday-101403.asp, accessed 25 September 2006.
3. See *Today Matters* (Nashville: Center Street, 2004) for the twelve areas I focus on and the habits I use daily to manage my life.
4. Cartoon copyright © 2010; reprinted courtesy of Bunny Hoest.
5. John C. Maxwell, *Leadership Gold* (Nashville: Thomas Nelson, 2008).
6. Cartoon copyright © 2001 by Randy Glasbergen.
7. "Gallup Study: Engaged Employees Inspire Company Innovation," *Gallup Management Journal,* 12 October 2006, http://gmj.gallup.com/content/24880/Gallup-Study-Engaged-Employees-Inspire-Company-Innovation.aspx; accessed 2 July 2010.
8. Marco Nink, "Employee Disengagement Plagues Germany," *Gallup Management Journal,* 9 April 2009, http://gmj.gallup.com/content/117376/Employee-Disengagement-Plagues-Germany.aspx; accessed 2 July 2010.

Level 2: Permission

1. Janet Lowe, *Jack Welch Speaks: Wit and Wisdom from the World's Greatest Business Leader* (New York: Wiley, 2007), 89.
2. Ibid.
3. "Active Listening," U.S. Department of State, http://www.state.gov/m/a/os/65759.htm; accessed 28 July 2010.

4. Martin Kalungu-Banda, *Leading like Madiba: Leadership Lessons from Nelson Mandela* (Cape Town, South Africa: Double Story Books, 2008), 13–15.
5. Bill Hybels and Mark Mittelberg, *Becoming a Contagious Christian* (Grand Rapids, MI: Zondervan, 1996), 57.
6. Warren Bennis and Burt Nanus, *Leaders: Strategies for Taking Charge* (New York: HarperBusiness, 1997), 52.
7. Matthew 7:12 (NKJV).
8. Hadith of an-Nawawi 13.
9. Talmud, Shabbat 31a, quoted in "The Universality of the Golden Rule in World Religions," www.teachingvalues.com, 23 September 2002.
10. Udana-Varga 5, 1, quoted in ibid.
11. Mahabharata 5, 1517, quoted in ibid.
12. Shast-na-shayast 13:29, quoted at www.thegoldenrule.net, 23 September 2002.
13. Analects 15:23, quoted at ibid.
14. Epistle to the Son of the Wolf, 30, quoted at www.fragrant.demon.co.uk/golden, 23 September 2002.
15. Sutrakritanga 1.11.33, quoted at ibid.
16. Ibid.
17. Proverbs 27:6 (NASB).
18. Pauline Graham, ed., *Mary Parker Follett: Prophet of Management* (Baltimore: Beard Books, 2003).

Level 3: Production

1. Joel Weldon, "Jobs Don't Have Futures, People Do," *The Unlimited Times* (e-newsletter), http://cmaanet.org/files/shared/CONTROLLABLES.pdf; accessed 19 August 2010.
2. Walt Mason, "The Welcome Man," in *It Can Be Done: Poems of Inspiration,* ed. Joseph Morris and St. Clair Adams (1921; Project Gutenberg, 2004), http://www.gutenberg.org/files/10763/10763-8.txt; accessed 19 August 2010.
3. Source unknown.
4. Jim Collins, *Good to Great: Why Some Companies Make the Leap...and Others Don't* (New York: HarperCollins, 2001), 139.
5. Henry Ford in interview *The American Magazine* (July 1928), vol. 106.

Level 4: People Development

1. Drucker, Peter, *On the Profession of Management* (Cambridge, MA: Harvard Business Review, 2003).

2. George Barna with Bill Dallas, *Master Leaders: Revealing Conversations with 30 Leadership Greats* (Carol Stream, IL: BarnaBooks, 2009), 61.

3. James A. Belasco and Ralph C. Stayer, *Flight of the Buffalo: Soaring to Excellence, Learning to Let Employees Lead* (New York: Warner Books, 1994), 19.

4. Everett Shostrom, *Man, The Manipulator* (New York: Bantam, 1980).

5. "The Little Boy and Sugar," Storytime for Children, Gandhi Memorial Center, Washington D.C., http://www.gandhimemorialcenter.org/for_children, accessed 8 April 2011.

6. George Barna with Bill Dallas, *Master Leaders* (Wheaton, IL: Tyndale, 2009), 62.

7. David Sedaris, *Naked* (New York: Back Bay Books, 1997), 215.

Level 5: The Pinnacle

1. Collins, *Good to Great*, 29.

2. Robert J. Thomas, "Crucibles of Leadership Development," *MIT Sloan Management Review* 49, no. 3 (Spring 2008), 15.

3. Ibid, 16.

Portrait of a Level 5 Leader

1. "John Wooden: A Coaching Legend, October 10, 1910—June 4, 2010," Official Website of UCLA Athletics, http://www.uclabruins.com/sports/m-baskbl/spec-rel/ucla-wooden-page.html; accessed 24 September 2010.

2. "John Wooden: Life and Times," UCLA, http://www.spotlight.ucla.edu/john-wooden/life-and-times; accessed 23 September 2010.

3. "NAIA Celebrates Black History Month—The Clarence Walker Story" (video), YouTube, http://www.youtube.com/watch?v=6TPw7UnCG3g; accessed 23 September 2010.

4. "John Wooden: A Coaching Legend."

5. "Season-by-Season Records," *UCLA History*, http://grfx.cstv.com/photos/schools/ucla/sports/m-baskbl/auto_pdf/MBB_History_99-128.pdf, 116; accessed 24 September 2010.

6. "John Wooden: A Coaching Legend."

7. "Sporting News' Top 50 Greatest Coaches of All Time," *Sporting News*, July 29, 2009, http://www.sportingnews.com/ncaa-basketball/story/2009-07-29/sporting-news-50-greatest-coaches-all-time; accessed 24 September 2010.

8. "Wooden's Pyramid of Success," The John R. Wooden Course, http://woodencourse.com/woodens_wisdom.html; accessed 24 September 2010.

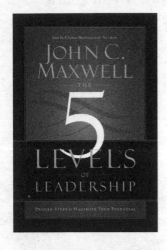
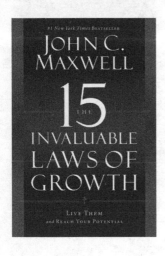